Discovering Apple Logo

Discovering Apple Logo

*An Invitation to the Art and
Pattern of Nature*

David D. Thornburg

ADDISON-WESLEY
PUBLISHING COMPANY

Reading, Massachusetts
Menlo Park, California   London   Amsterdam
Don Mills, Ontario   Sydney

This book is in the **Addison-Wesley Microcomputer Books** Popular Series

Thomas A. Bell, *Sponsoring Editor*
Marshall Henrichs, *Cover Design*
Ellen Klempner, *Design*

Apple is a registered trademark of Apple Computer, Inc.

Second Printing, October 1983

Library of Congress Cataloging in Publication Data
Thornburg, David D.
Discovering Apple Logo

(Addison-Wesley and microcomputer books popular
series)
Bibliography: p.
1. Logo (Computer program language) 2. Apple II
(Computer)—Programming. 3. Computer graphics.
4. Geometry—Data processing. I. Title. II. Series.
QA76.73.L63T48 1983   001.64′24   82-20704
ISBN 0-201-07769-8

ISBN 0-201-07769-8
BCDEFGHIJ-HA-89876543

The flowers appear on the earth; the time of the singing of the birds is come, and the voice of the turtle is heard in our land . . .

The Song of Solomon 2:12

Preface

Discovering Apple Logo is a book that deals with three topics—graphic art, geometry, and computer programming—as though they were braided together into one cord. At any point in this book, one thread may be more visible than the others, yet I have endeavored to interrelate them in a coherent, meaningful way.

It is not expected that readers of this book are expert artists, mathematicians, or computer programmers. It is hoped, however, that if readers are interested in at least one of these topics, the text will help them make enjoyable discoveries in the other two fields.

For many reasons, the computer language Logo has been chosen as the programming environment for this book. Logo is an exceptionally powerful language whose syntax allows it to be learned easily by people who have had no previous experience with computers. Seymour Papert's *Mindstorms: Children, Computers and Powerful Ideas* describes both the motivation behind this language and its enthusiastic reception by neophyte computer users of all ages.

Because of Logo's extraordinary power, it has only recently been possible to implement this language on small, personal-scale computer systems. The particular implementation of Logo with which we shall be concerned is the version for the Apple II computer designed by LOGO Computer Systems, Inc., and sold by Apple Computer, Inc. Other versions of Logo exist—both for the Apple and for other computers, such as Texas Instrument's 99/4 personal computer.

As with natural languages, regional dialects occur in the development of computer languages. Although this book will concentrate on a particular implementation of Logo, readers who have other versions of this language for the Apple (for example, the Terrapin Logo Language) or TI Logo should find that much of the material will be useful without modification.

Much of the excitement surrounding Logo is a result of its incorporation of a beautifully simple and powerful graphics environment. Pictures are created on the display screen by giving instructions to an imaginary "turtle," which draws lines as it moves along. These instructions take the form of a descriptive procedure of the object being drawn. As this book is devoted primarily to "turtle graphics," it is perhaps beneficial to compare the turtle's characteristics to those of conventional coordinate geometry.

In familiar (Cartesian) planar geometry, the location of a point in a plane is specified by its coordinates (usually denoted by the letters x and y). The x coordinate measures the point's position from a vertical reference line, and the y coordinate measures the point's distance above (or below) a horizontal reference line.

Another way of describing the properties of a point is to specify its *orientation* as well as its x and y coordinates. There are several reasons why this additional piece of information is valuable. First, it allows simple representation of a graphic object through a procedure that, when followed, will generate the object. For example, if our point (which we will call the turtle) is pointing straight up, we can describe a 50-unit square by the following set of instructions:

FORWARD 50 (*units*)
RIGHT 90 (*degrees*)
FORWARD 50
RIGHT 90
FORWARD 50
RIGHT 90
FORWARD 50
RIGHT 90

Aside from the utility of this type of representation in developing an intuition for geometry, an even more compelling reason to be interested in this descriptive process is that it is simple yet extremely powerful. Consider the following two responses to the question "Where do you live?"

Response 1:   "I live at 1234 Snowflake Court."
Response 2:   "You go down this street for two blocks, turn right, and go down three houses to the one with the blue door and the oak tree in front."

The first response, an address measured against a fixed reference, assumes familiarity with the streets in an area perhaps as large as a city. To make use of that answer, you also have to know where Snowflake Court is relative to your present location. Although the address might be complete, it is only valuable to you if you are familiar with the city. The second response describes the procedure by which you would get to the house, given your present position and orientation. It is a purely "local" description in that it makes no assumption that you know any of the streets in the community. It assumes only that you can follow simple instructions that make incremental changes in your present position. If you were in a strange city, you probably would find the second answer much more useful than the first. Each instruction is given with respect to the position and orientation of the participant at the end of the previous instruction. This descriptive procedure is identical to that used in turtle graphics.

Just as descriptive procedures make sense, the exceptional power of turtle graphics makes it most valuable for illustrating important properties of geometric figures (for example, curvature). Its similarity to natural descriptive language has made turtle graphics a most powerful vehicle in allowing people to discover important geometric principles on their own.

My first exposure to turtle graphics came when I worked at the Xerox Palo Alto Research Center—the home of the language SMALLTALK. Although SMALLTALK supports an exceptional turtle graphics environment, it was implemented on computer systems that were far too expensive for the average consumer. I have used several turtle environments over the years, including computer languages such as WSFN (Which Stands For Nothing) and "toys" such as Milton Bradley's Big Trak. The turtle environments in the languages Atari PILOT and Apple SuperPILOT are the subject matter of two of my other books: *Picture This!* and *Picture This Too!* This book, however, is concerned only with the language Logo. The simplicity and exceptional power of this language allows the user to concentrate on the application of the language rather than on the language's structure. As a result, the reader will find the computer to be a comfortable tool of discovery—not a time-consuming object of study.

My experience has shown that, whatever the form—an actual robot or a graphic display—turtle environments are liked especially by people who previously have been afraid to learn how to program a computer. If you have never worked with a computer before (and you have access to a computer that uses Logo), you will find this book to be a most gentle guide to a very powerful tool.

I have been encouraged to write books in this area by many members of the research, product design, and development community who are actively generating user-friendly languages. Apple Computer, Inc., has been particularly supportive of this present project.

It is a pleasure to acknowledge my debt to those who have labored long and hard to develop user-friendly computer languages. I am also indebted to my friends in the computer graphics community—particularly Scott Kim and Howard Pearlmutter—for their willingness to provide me with a kind ear, spirited discussions, and an occasional forum for the expression of my fondness for the turtle.

Most of all, I am indebted to the children and artists with whom I have shared my efforts in this area over the past few years. Were it not for the joyful inquisitiveness of these people, this book would not exist.

Los Altos, California   D.T.
January 1983

Contents

I.

Introduction: Patterns, Mathematics, and Computers

If I knew what two and two were—
I would say Four!

Saying of the Mulla Nasrudin
(from The Subtleties of the Inimitable
Mulla Nasrudin, **Idries Shah)**

What This Book Is All About

This is a book about discovery—the discovery each of us can make when finding beauty in geometric patterns, beauty in mathematics, and beauty in computer programming.

It is easy to see how one might find beauty in geometric patterns; this beauty forms the foundation of nature and art. We are continually entranced by geometric form—the symmetry of a butterfly's wings, the spiral of a snail's shell, the facets of a crystal—and each of these natural occurrences is perceived as having beauty associated with it. The hands of people have produced geometric art since marks were first made on cave walls or stones were first fashioned into tools. From the Pyramids and the Parthenon to the finest gold-link chain, the beauty of geometric form is clearly present for all who care to find it.

Underlying the geometric pattern that we experience with our eyes lies a more subtle pattern of mathematical beauty, which is experienced intellectually—a collection of unifying principles that govern the arrangement and shapes of objects, both natural and crafted. To glimpse this power of mathematics, con-

sider four regular geometric figures—a triangle, a square, a pentagon, and a hexagon.

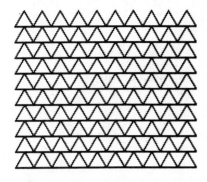

Each of these simple polygons has sides of equal length. Suppose you wanted to make a tile floor using polygons of only one type. You can tile a floor with triangles.

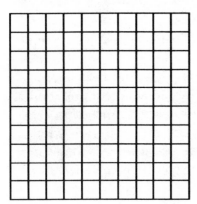

You can tile a floor with squares.

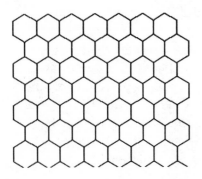

And you can tile a floor with hexagons.

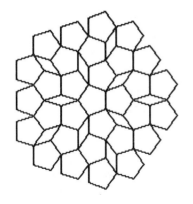

However, no matter how hard you try, you cannot tile a floor with regular pentagons.

Why is this? The answer to this question is found in a beautiful mathematical discovery of a unifying property that applies to all shapes that can be drawn on a flat surface. This concept (and many more) will be explored in this book.

Along with the beauty of form and mathematics, there is another beauty we will explore—the beauty of descriptive procedures that use mathematical concepts to create pictures of our geometric forms on a computer display screen. Through these descriptive procedures we can command the computer to generate an unlimited array of pictures, many of which we might find nearly impossible to create with any other medium.

You might wonder how an electrical device as complex and technical as a computer can be an effective tool for creative expression. Many people who have avoided using computers have done so for a variety of reasons. Some feel that you have to be "good at math" to use a computer. Some feel that a computer is useful only for balancing checkbooks or for performing other tasks that are clearly defined in advance. Some feel that the computer is so hard to use that by the time you have learned how, you have forgotten what you wanted to do with it in the first place.

These ideas can be dispelled as myths. Whatever the computer has been before, it is now also something else. The computer today can be a tool for discovery and creative expression. It can be as moldable as a piece of clay and as powerful as the very ideas it helps to express.

To get full benefit from this book, you should have access to a computer system that uses the language Logo. This language is available for the Apple II computer, among others. All the program examples in this book were written in Apple Logo, although they should work with many other Logo systems as well. In the remainder of this chapter we will trace the events that brought the power of this programming environment into people's homes.

Computers for People

Fifteen years ago, computers were very hard to use. First you had to spend a lot of time learning to write computer programs in a language that was specialized for your application. If you were a scientist or engineer, you might use a computer language called FORTRAN (FORmula TRANslation). If your application was business related, you might use COBOL (COmmon Business Oriented Language). Once you learned the language, you would then generate the program statements for the problem you wanted to solve. Next, you would have to punch these commands onto special cards, which you then carried to a computer center. Here you would pass your stack of cards to a highly trained computer operator, who would place your task in line with hundreds of other jobs being performed by a massive central computer. If you were lucky, you could pick up the results of your program an hour or so later. The massive computer probably spent less than a few seconds performing the tasks you requested; the time delay was caused by one central computer serving the needs of many users.

This mode of computer usage is not very inviting to those who would like to experiment with programming. In fact, the only people who used computers 15 years ago were those who were highly motivated to do so. Whatever computing was then, it certainly was not casual.

Attempts to make the central computer more responsive to the needs of its users resulted in the creation of "time-sharing" systems. In the time-sharing environment a central computer was connected by telephone lines to computer terminals located in each user's office. For the first time, this allowed interaction between the user and the computer while the computer was working on the user's task. Although time sharing greatly increased people's access to computers, it was a pale compromise when compared to the revolution that happened next.

A most important year in the development of computers was 1978. It was then that affordable small computer systems were first being sold to people who had had no previous experience with them.

The development of the personal computer promises to have an impact as great as that of the automobile. Millions of these small computers are being used for everything from games to business, education, and communication. There seems to be no limit to the application of the personal computer; and yet, until quite recently, the revolution was incomplete.

For the computer to be truly useful, it needed to be easily programmable by its user. Furthermore, although the programming language had to be easy to use, it also needed to have sufficient power to allow its continued use as the user became more proficient. It was the development of powerful user-friendly computer languages that formed the basis for the second revolution.

Languages for People to Use with Computers

The function of language is to aid communication. Communication implies the interchange of ideas or expressions between two or more parties. If I talk to you in English, you probably will understand what I say. If you talk to me in Swahili, I will not understand you, because Swahili is not a language I speak. In order to be useful for communication, a language has to be shared by all parties.

How do we pick languages for computers? At one extreme, we could send the computer the patterns of 1's and 0's that form the elements of its computational framework. Although this language of the machine may make it work effectively, it is so different from natural languages that it is a poor choice. On the other extreme, we might choose a language such as English. Although this would seem to simplify our task, English is too imprecise to serve effectively as a computer language. Consider, for example, the phrase *pretty little girl's school*. Does this refer to a school for pretty little girls, to a pretty school for little girls, or to something else altogether?

It is far better to devise computer languages that form intermediate compromises between these extremes. The interactive computer language BASIC (Beginner's All-purpose Symbolic Instruction Code) was the principal programming environment for the first few years of the personal computer revolution. BASIC was well suited for this task because it used English language "keywords" to instruct the computer to perform well-defined tasks. By using words in carefully defined, nonambiguous ways, it became possible for the user to generate his or her own programs. But certain characteristics of BASIC showed that its days were numbered.

Like natural languages, computer languages have rules of grammar and vocabularies. The rules of grammar are fairly rigidly fixed for most languages, but BASIC also has a fixed vocabulary. The restriction implied by a fixed vocabulary is quite severe. Imagine how effective English would be if, for example, no new words had entered the language since the time of Shakespeare. What would we call computers, televisions, or automobiles?

For natural languages to survive, they must be extensible; new words must be able to enter the language as they are needed. The vitality this extensibility gives to natural languages also applies to computer languages. For example, because BASIC programmers are forced to live with a fixed vocabulary, a skilled BASIC programmer will find that the language becomes quite cumbersome for the expression of sophisticated programming ideas.

Research on extensible computer languages has been conducted in university and industrial research centers for many years. Central to these new languages is the idea that the user should be able to use carefully defined primitive instructions to build new commands into the language and then give those new functions their own names.

One language of this new type is called Logo. The complex problem of translating this language into the fundamental commands used by the computer restricted its use to large computer systems until very recently. In 1981 Logo first became available on a low-cost personal computer—the Texas Instruments 99/4. Within a year, several versions of this language also appeared for the Apple II computer. It is the Apple version in which the examples in this book were created.

Logo is easily the most powerful and user-friendly computer language ever implemented on a personal computer. It has an extraordinarily powerful graphics environment (whose characteristics will be amply illustrated in this book); it can be used with very little formal instruction; and it can be extended by the user as desired.

The power of Logo must be experienced to be believed. Many people who are familiar with other languages embrace Logo as being the best computer language they have seen. As you work with Logo yourself, you may see why the enthusiasm for this language is so great.

II.

Logo and the Turtle: A Gentle Guide to a Powerful Language

"When we were little . . . we went to school in the sea. The master was an old Turtle—we used to call him Tortoise." "Why did you call him Tortoise if he wasn't one?" Alice asked. "We called him Tortoise because he taught us," said the Mock Turtle angrily. "Really, you are very dense."

Alice's Adventures in Wonderland

To get full benefit from this book, you will need to have access to a computer system that uses the language Logo. Although this language is available for several popular small computers, we will focus our attention on the version for the Apple II or II+ computer system. If you have an Apple computer but do not yet have Logo, your local dealer can provide you with everything you need.

We will assume that your computer is equipped with a color video display and one disk drive. Although color lets you add another dimension to your pictures, it isn't necessary for anything we will do, and you can get along just as well with a black-and-white display.

The disk drive is an essential part of your computer system. First, it is the tool that lets your computer retrieve Logo from the language disk. Second, it lets you store your Logo projects on your own disk for later use. The Logo language disk is set up only to let the computer load information from it. Your own disk will allow the computer to save information and to load it back at another time. The manuals accompanying your copy of Apple Logo tell you how to initialize your own disk. You will probably want to do this soon, although it won't be necessary for a while.

The rest of this chapter is devoted to the basic mechanics of getting Logo started on the computer and to the basic characteristics and commands of the graphics system. If you are already familiar with these topics, you may skip to the next chapter if you wish.

Getting Started with Apple Logo

To start your system, make sure that the disk drive, television set (or monitor), and all the rest of your Apple computer system is properly set up. Next, turn on your television set or monitor and insert your Logo language disk into the disk drive (your manuals show you how). Close the latch on the disk drive, and turn the computer on. If everything is working, the red light on the disk drive will turn on and you will hear a whirring sound. After a brief pause, the following message will appear on the screen:

PRESS THE RETURN KEY TO BEGIN
IF YOU HAVE YOUR OWN FILE DISKETTE,
INSERT IT NOW, THEN PRESS RETURN

© LOGO COMPUTER SYSTEMS INC. 1982

If you don't see this message, turn the computer off and make sure that the disk is properly inserted before trying again.

When you see this message, you have three options. You can press the RETURN key, you can replace the language disk with your own file disk if you wish, or you can start Logo immediately by holding down the key marked CTRL and pressing the G key. You can use this sequence of keystrokes (called control-G) whenever you want to interrupt what Logo is doing. If you leave the language disk in place and press the key marked RETURN, the screen will go blank, and the red light on the disk drive will blink on and off as additional files are loaded into the Apple's memory. When this task is finished, the screen will show the following message:

WELCOME TO LOGO   A1.5
?

The flashing square that appears after the question mark is called the *text cursor*. It shows where a character will appear if you press one of the keys. Try typing something like

HELLO

and notice how the cursor moves along as you type. You are creating a message to send to your computer. To send this message, press the RETURN key. As soon as you do this, the computer will display this message:

I DON'T KNOW HOW TO HELLO

and present you with a fresh question mark.

Well, the computer doesn't appear to understand our greeting; but we did learn something very important. To send commands to the computer, you must press the RETURN key after you have typed the instructions you want the computer to follow. Later you may find that you will type instructions that are more than one line long. In this case you will keep on typing until you are done and then press the RETURN key at the very end, rather than at the end of each line of text on the screen.

So far we have been viewing what Logo refers to

as the **TEXTSCREEN**. This screen can display up to 24 lines of text, each of which is up to 40 characters in length.

Logo has two other types of display screens that we will use. To see one of them, we send the computer a special command by typing the word

SPLITSCREEN

and (did you remember?) pressing the RETURN key. If, as you were typing, you typed something wrong (**SPILTSCREEN**, for example) you can fix the mistake *before* pressing RETURN by pressing the DELETE key to erase the incorrect letters. The DELETE key is marked with an arrow pointing to the left. When you have deleted the incorrect characters, retype the rest of the command and press the RETURN key.

As soon as Logo receives the message **SPLIT-SCREEN**, the display changes quite a bit. The question mark and text cursor appear near the bottom of the screen, and a white triangular object appears in the center of the screen.

When you give Logo the **SPLITSCREEN** command, you are directing the computer to let you see up to four lines of text. The rest of the screen is devoted to graphics. By sending the appropriate message to the triangular object in the middle of the screen, you can have it draw pictures on the display. The triangular object is called the *turtle*. We will learn all about the turtle soon, but first we need to learn more about the space in which the turtle moves.

Since **TEXTSCREEN** displays all text (try entering this command and see for yourself), and **SPLIT-SCREEN** shows both text and graphics, it is logical to expect that there is a command that presents you with a pure graphics display. To see this screen, type **FULLSCREEN** and press RETURN. Now all you will see on the screen is the turtle. Even though you can't see what you are typing, Logo is paying attention to the keyboard. To see this, type TEXTSCREEN and press RETURN. You should now be back to your original screen.

Practice switching between TEXTSCREEN, SPLITSCREEN, and FULLSCREEN a few times to be sure you know how to do it.

Introducing the Turtle

The turtle is a powerful Logo object that lets us draw pictures on the display screen. It is convenient to think of the turtle as a robot to which we send commands. The two most important types of commands at our disposal are those that make the turtle move in a straight line and those that make the turtle turn. By using combinations of these commands, we can instruct the turtle to draw almost anything we wish on the display. The pictures are drawn by a "pen" that is carried by the turtle. We can change the pen color, lift it up, set it down, and change the pen to an eraser. When the turtle first starts out, it is holding a white pen that is "down" (ready to draw).

To make the turtle draw a line, first instruct Logo to set up the SPLITSCREEN. When you see both the turtle and the question mark with the text cursor next to it, enter

FORWARD 50

As soon as you press RETURN, the turtle will draw a line from its starting (home) position to a point 50 units away.

Next, try entering the command

LEFT 90

As soon as you press RETURN, the turtle will turn 90 degrees to the left.

If you now type

FORWARD 100

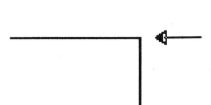

the turtle will move forward in its new direction.

How far can the turtle move? To find out, let's have the turtle draw some more in the same direction. Enter

FORWARD 100

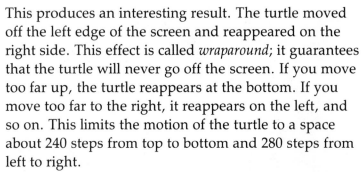

This produces an interesting result. The turtle moved off the left edge of the screen and reappeared on the right side. This effect is called *wraparound*; it guarantees that the turtle will never go off the screen. If you move too far up, the turtle reappears at the bottom. If you move too far to the right, it reappears on the left, and so on. This limits the motion of the turtle to a space about 240 steps from top to bottom and 280 steps from left to right.

There are times when we would rather have the turtle be able to move off the screen rather than wrap around to the other side. To see how to do this, first type

CLEARSCREEN

As soon as you press RETURN, the screen will be cleared and the turtle will be put back to the home position and orientation (at the center of the screen and facing straight up). Next, enter

WINDOW

Nothing seems to change, and yet if you enter

FORWARD 500

the turtle will move off the screen.

To bring the turtle into its home position once again, enter

BACK 500

See, it isn't lost after all!

Next enter

RIGHT 90
FORWARD 500

and then

BACK 500

to convince yourself that **WINDOW** removes the screen limits for the turtle. To go back to the original wraparound screen, just enter

WRAP

(and press RETURN).

At this point we should summarize the Logo commands that pertain to the display screen.

TEXTSCREEN —creates a screen that shows up to 24 lines of 40 characters each.

SPLITSCREEN —creates a screen that shows turtle graphics in the upper five-sixths of the screen and four lines of text near the bottom.

FULLSCREEN —creates a full screen for the turtle graphics.

WRAP —keeps the turtle on the display screen by having it reappear from the edge opposite the one it moved past.

WINDOW —allows the turtle to be moved off the screen.

We have also found some of the basic commands that make the turtle move around the screen:

CLEARSCREEN —erases the graphics display, places the turtle back in the home location at the center of the screen, and points the turtle to face straight up.

FORWARD *x* —moves the turtle forward in its present heading by *x* units.

BACK *x* —moves the turtle backward in its present heading by *x* units.

RIGHT *x* —turns the turtle to the right by *x* degrees.

LEFT *x* —turns the turtle to the left by *x* degrees.

These last four commands are particularly important because (as we will see later) they allow us to easily create procedures by which the computer can draw any figure of interest to us.

Before moving on to the creation of figures, we should first learn about a few more primitive graphics commands. CLEARSCREEN, for example, does two things: it erases whatever has been drawn on the display and it moves the turtle to its home location and orientation. Suppose that we only want to perform one of these tasks—clean off the screen or move the turtle home. How would we do this? Logo provides two special commands for just this purpose. To see how they work, enter

CLEARSCREEN
FORWARD 50
RIGHT 45
FORWARD 50

This draws two lines on the screen.

Now note the location and orientation of the turtle and enter

CLEAN

As soon as you press RETURN, the picture is erased, but the turtle stays in the same place.

Next, enter

HOME

This causes the turtle to move in a straight line to its home position. Since the pen was down at the time, it also drew a line. As you can see, the turtle not only is at the center of the screen but is also pointing straight up. The command CLEARSCREEN performs the same function as the two-command combination HOME CLEAN.

Next, let's learn how to make the turtle do some more things with the pen, such as pick it up, change its color, and so on. Recall that when the turtle first starts out, it is holding a white pen in the down (drawing) position. To see how to move this pen up and down, try the following. Enter

CLEARSCREEN
FORWARD 50
PENUP
RIGHT 90
FORWARD 50
PENDOWN
FORWARD 50

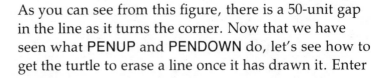

As you can see from this figure, there is a 50-unit gap in the line as it turns the corner. Now that we have seen what PENUP and PENDOWN do, let's see how to get the turtle to erase a line once it has drawn it. Enter

CLEARSCREEN
FORWARD 100

to draw a line on the screen. Now, to erase it, enter

PENERASE
BACK 100

and, presto, the original line is erased. To draw a line again, just enter

PENDOWN
FORWARD 100

So far, we have worked with a white pen against a black background. Logo lets us change pen and background colors independently. Because of the way your Apple computer displays colors, the pen colors you use may appear different against different background colors. You should experiment with this phenomenon to see it for yourself.

To set the pen to a new color, just enter the command

SETPC *x*

where *x* is a number from 0 to 5. Each number corresponds to a color shown in following table:

COMMAND	COLOR
SETPC 0	black
SETPC 1	white
SETPC 2	green
SETPC 3	violet
SETPC 4	orange
SETPC 5	blue

To try this out, enter

CLEARSCREEN
SETPC 2
FORWARD 50
RIGHT 90
SETPC 3
FORWARD 50
RIGHT 90
SETPC 4
FORWARD 50
RIGHT 90
SETPC 5
FORWARD 50
RIGHT 90

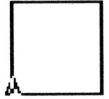

This will give you a multicolored square on the screen.

To see something really exciting, enter the following commands:

SETBG 1
SETBG 2
SETBG 3
SETBG 4
SETBG 5
SETBG 0

As you enter each line, the background color changes on the display screen. If you look closely, you will notice that the lines of the square change color too. SETBG is the command that changes the background color. It uses the same color table as SETPC, with one exception: SETBG 6 gives a black background, which is perfect if you are using a black-and-white display, since it lets the pen draw thinner lines than it can with the normal background color, SETBG 0. However, SETBG 6 doesn't let you draw colored lines, so it isn't very useful if you have a color display.

Before concluding this chapter, we have a magic trick for the turtle to perform. Ready? Enter

CLEARSCREEN

You can see the turtle in the middle of the screen. Next, enter

HIDETURTLE

and, *poof*, the turtle becomes invisible. You can convince yourself that the turtle is still there by having it draw some lines. To see the turtle again, enter

SHOWTURTLE

You may want to keep the turtle visible while you are learning how to use the turtle graphics. Once you are comfortable with this graphics environment, you will probably want to make the turtle invisible so that it doesn't interfere with your drawing. An added benefit is that lines are drawn faster when the turtle is hidden.

Because of our emphasis on graphics, you may be thinking that Logo is primarily a graphics language. Nothing could be further from the truth. As we progress through this book, other aspects of Logo will be presented as well.

We packed a tremendous amount of information into this chapter, so you might want to experiment some more with these commands and instructions before going on. Above all, don't feel that you have to commit this chapter to memory before proceeding. The best way to learn Logo is to use it.

III. Lines and Figures: The Turtle Moves On

Beauty is the harmony and concord of all parts, achieved in such a manner that nothing could be taken away or altered except for the worse.

Leon Battista Alberti (1404–1472)

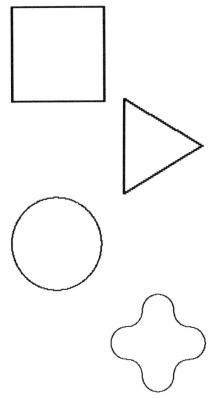

Each of the four figures here has something in common with the others.

They are all closed figures. This means that each has a boundary that separates its inside from its outside. The first two figures (the square and the triangle) are examples of regular polygons. The third figure is a circle, and the last is a meandering curve that produces a closed figure.

It is common to think of such patterns in a static way—a way that describes their existence as completed objects. In reality, however, any figure or form is created by a *process*—a sequence of events that moves from the universe without the expression of the figure to the universe with the figure in it. Since nothing in nature can happen instantaneously, anything that exists does so by virtue of the process that created it. When we see only the finished form, we often lose the information used in its creation. This information is often as interesting as the final form itself.

What is less obvious is that a description of the process by which an object is created can be a more succinct and understandable representation of the object than a description based on the final form alone. As we embark on our exploration of the generative processes for various forms, you will have ample opportunity to test this hypothesis for yourself.

A Closed Path

If we start with the turtle in the center of the screen (by typing CLEARSCREEN, for example), we can generate a picture of a square by having the turtle draw a continuous line as it moves in a square path. Each of the figures here shows the result of each successive instruction obeyed by the turtle.

```
FORWARD 80
RIGHT 90
FORWARD 80
RIGHT 90
FORWARD 80
RIGHT 90
FORWARD 80
RIGHT 90
```

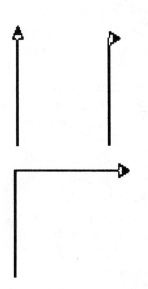

[NOTE: If the image on your display screen looks rectangular rather than square, you can have Logo compensate for your display's aspect ratio by using the SETSCRUNCH command. When you first load Logo into the computer, the ratio of vertical to horizontal step size is set at 0.8. This value compensates properly for most television sets. If your image is too wide, try typing SETSCRUNCH 1 and redrawing the picture. If the image is too narrow, use a lower value in SETSCRUNCH and try again. Make note of the value that works for you and remember to use SET-SCRUNCH with this value each time you start using the computer.]

If you look at the last two figures in the series we just drew, you can see that they are both squares. The

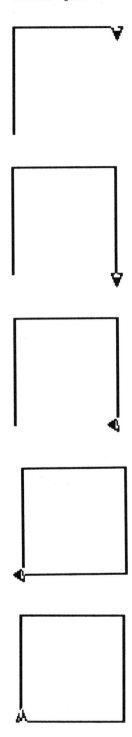

major difference between them has to do with the orientation of the turtle. In the next to last figure, the turtle is in its starting position but is pointing to the left. In the last figure, the turtle is in both its starting position and its starting orientation. By returning to the exact location and orientation from which we have started, we have sent the turtle around a perfectly closed path.

Closed paths of this type are called *state change invariant* because they return the turtle to its exact starting position. These paths have some interesting properties, which will be explored in the next chapter. Meanwhile, let's examine a shorter way of having Logo create figures of this type.

The instructions we used to create the square consisted of the commands **FORWARD 80** and **RIGHT 90**, repeated four times. Logo has a special command that makes it easy for us to write repeated expressions. To create a square quickly, clear the screen and enter

REPEAT 4 [FORWARD 80 RIGHT 90]

(To enter the left and right square brackets, hold down the SHIFT key and press the N key for the left bracket and the M key for the right.) As soon as this line is entered and you press RETURN, you will see the square drawn on the display screen. For the **REPEAT** command to work, it needs two pieces of information: a number telling how many times to repeat something and a list of commands to repeat. In Logo all lists are enclosed in square brackets. Lists are very powerful tools for storing data, and much of Logo's power derives from its ability to work with lists. Later we will see other ways in which lists are useful.

Now let's examine our compact description of a square:

REPEAT 4 [FORWARD 80 RIGHT 90]

The process that is described by this statement conveys the *essence* of a square, since a square has four equal sides and four equal angles (of 90 degrees each). This procedure provides us with a purely local description of a square. The same procedure will generate a square from any starting location and orientation of the turtle. To see this, we can use the Logo command SETPOS to set the position of the turtle to other screen locations from which we can draw squares. The SETPOS command needs information in the form of a list of horizontal (*x*) and vertical (*y*) coordinates for the turtle. For example, enter

CLEARSCREEN
REPEAT 4 [FORWARD 50 RIGHT 90]

to see a square drawn from the turtle's home position.

Next, enter

PENUP
SETPOS [−60 −20]
PENDOWN

to move the turtle to a new location.

Then use the same command sequence for the square:

REPEAT 4 [FORWARD 50 RIGHT 90]

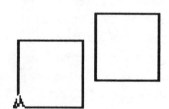

Now let's change the pen color to orange, rotate the turtle by 30 degrees, and draw the square again:

SETPC 4
RIGHT 30
REPEAT 4 [FORWARD 50 RIGHT 90]

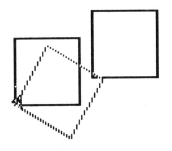

This example illustrates the fact that the command

REPEAT 4 [FORWARD 50 RIGHT 90]

describes a 50-unit square at any turtle location or orientation. The beauty of the process descriptions we will use is that they describe the properties of the objects we are creating independently from the locations of these objects in space.

Before discovering some other properties of procedures that generate closed figures, we will digress to a topic that is relevant to all geometric forms—symmetry.

Symmetry

Patterns—whether natural or handmade—often have a repetitive underlying structure that we call symmetry. These three figures will help to illustrate different ways that figures can be symmetrical.

If you were to group these figures on the basis of what they have in common, you would probably group the star with the spiral and exclude the random scribble shown in the last figure. The star and the spiral are similar in that they were both generated by a completely determined rule that could be deduced by studying the finished figures. The random scribble wasn't the result of any such rule.

Both the star and the spiral are symmetrical figures, although each has a different kind of symmetry. Looking at the star, we can see that it was made by repeating a subunit five times. This subunit drew a line and turned by some angle. Because each of these subunits was the same—both in the length of the line and in the turning angle—the resulting figure has a rotational symmetry. If you were to make a star of the same size and lay it over the one in the figure, you would find five rotational positions at which the two stars would overlap perfectly. The star has fivefold rotational symmetry. Using the same process, you can

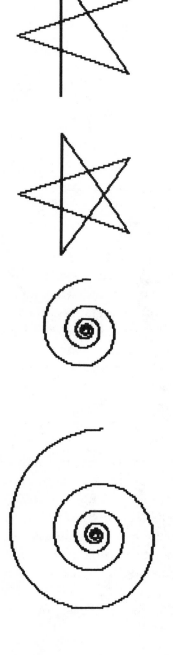

convince yourself that a square has fourfold rotational symmetry and that a rectangle has twofold rotational symmetry.

Complete figures, such as the star, have a very important property. As the star was being made, it went from a point of incompletion to the point at which it was finished. At most stages of its development it was not a star; then, at the end, it finally became a star.

Prior to the last step, we did not have a figure that had the symmetry or form of the final result. Only when the last step was taken was the star finished. At this point no additional lines could be added without changing the nature of the figure.

We will refer to figures of this type as figures displaying *static symmetry*. Static symmetry is found in snowflakes, mineral crystals, floor tiles, wallpaper patterns, and myriad other objects that we can call complete or finished.

The spiral is an example of a figure displaying a different kind of symmetry. The spiral is sufficiently well organized that we can deduce the procedure for its creation by studying the spiral itself. Even without knowing this procedure explicitly, you probably could continue to extend it yourself, based on the portion already present.

The symmetry displayed by the spiral is one of proportion. Each segment of the spiral arm is proportionately related to the preceding section. The spiral is always ready to grow; there is never a point at which it becomes complete.

One consequence of this is that the spiral has a property called *handedness*. Our spiral grows by turning to the right, and thus is called a right-handed spiral.

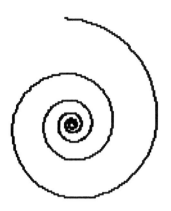

We can just as easily create a left-handed spiral.

Because figures of this type are never finished, we will call them figures of *dynamic symmetry*. Dynamic symmetry is found in sea shells, flowers, pinecones, whirlpools, woven baskets, and in many other objects that can be enlarged proportionately by repeating the same process that created the object in the first place. As we progress through this book, we will explore many examples of both static and dynamic symmetry.

IV.

Paths and Procedures

And then there was Rose.

Rose was her name and would she have been Rose if her name had not been Rose. She used to think and then she used to think again.

Would she have been Rose if her name had not been Rose and would she have been Rose if she had been a twin.

(from The World is Round, **Gertrude Stein)**

As we mentioned in Chapter I, the power of natural languages derives from their ability to be extended. Imagine how useless English would be if no new words were introduced to the language since the time of Shakespeare. What would we call televisions, telephones, automobiles, or computers? Natural languages are extended as a result of people's needs to express thoughts whose expression is too cumbersome for the existing vocabulary.

A computer language that is extensible has two features. First, the user benefits from being able to re-place complex definitions by a single word, which then becomes part of the computer's lexicon. Second, extensibility allows the language designer to focus on the primitive commands from which new words can be defined. By not focusing on the wealth of applications for which the language may be applied, the primitive commands can be combined into new procedures by each user, who in effect creates a personal version of the language, tailored to his or her specific needs and interests.

Simple Procedures

All the commands we have used thus far are Logo primitives. The creation of extensions to Logo occurs through the definition of *procedures*. Suppose, for example, that we wanted to have the turtle draw a 50-unit square in response to the word SQUARE. If you enter this word now, you will probably see the following message:

I DON'T KNOW HOW TO SQUARE

This message lets you know that SQUARE is not a word in Logo's dictionary of procedures. To change this, enter the following:

TO SQUARE
REPEAT 4 [FORWARD 50 RIGHT 90]
END

When you press RETURN after entering the first line, the prompt symbol changes from a question mark to an angle bracket ()). This symbol lets us know that Logo is adding the following lines to the definition of the procedure SQUARE. All Logo procedures must finish with the command END. As soon as you enter END and press RETURN, Logo prints the message

SQUARE DEFINED

and returns to the original question mark prompt. Any time you see the question mark prompt on the screen, Logo will attempt to execute any commands you enter. When you define a new procedure (by using the command TO followed by the name of the procedure), the screen shows the angle bracket at the beginning of each line until you enter the word **END**. Anything you enter while the angle bracket is visible will be entered into the definition of the procedure.

[NOTE: As an alternative to this method of procedure definition, Logo has a powerful built-in editor that lets you create procedures and modify them easily (to correct errors, and so on). You should refer to your Logo manuals to learn how to use this editor; it will save you a lot of time. In the remainder of the book we will just list procedures without specifying how you are to enter them.]

To see if Logo now "knows" about the word **SQUARE**, enter

```
CLEARSCREEN
SQUARE
```

When you press RETURN after entering **SQUARE**, a 50-unit square appears on the screen. Thus the Logo language has just been extended to include the procedure **SQUARE**.

This procedure can now be treated just as if it were a primitive command. For example, try to anticipate what this command will do:

```
CLEARSCREEN
REPEAT 6 [SQUARE RIGHT 60]
```

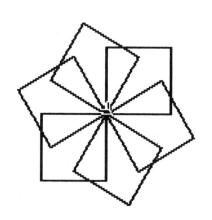

Now that you know how to extend Logo, you should know how to save your extensions so that you won't have to re-create them each time you use the computer. To save all of your procedures, place an initialized file diskette in the disk drive (your Logo manuals show you how to prepare such a diskette) and enter

```
SAVE "SQUAREFILE
```

When you press RETURN, all your procedures will be saved on the diskette in a file whose name is the word SQUAREFILE. Although I picked SQUAREFILE, you can use any word you wish for the file name. Since this is the fourth chapter of the book, you might want to use the word CHAPT4, for example. Since you will end up with quite a few files on your disk, it is a good idea to pick file names that give a clue as to their contents. To avoid confusion, it is also a good idea to use a file name that is not the same as the name of any procedure in the file.

[NOTE: In Logo, *words* are collections of letters and numbers with no spaces between them. The quotation mark used in the SAVE command must precede the word you are going to use. Just as Logo requires that all *lists* be enclosed in square brackets, it requires that all *words* be preceded by a quotation mark.]

To see the names of the procedures saved on your diskette, just enter

CATALOG

and the screen will display the names of the files as well as information regarding their size. You will probably notice that the file names have been extended by the suffix .LOGO. This is just a bit of bookkeeping information to label the file type; it is not a part of the file name that you will need to use for anything.

If you turn your Apple off and restart Logo, you will find that it has no recollection of the meaning of the procedure named SQUARE. If, however, you next enter

LOAD "SQUAREFILE

the procedures in this file will be brought into the computer. Once this is done, you can again use the procedure **SQUARE**.

Before moving on to some other topics, we should finish our discussion of procedures and files with a description of a few more commands. Suppose that you create a few more procedures that you wish to save in the file named **SQUAREFILE**. If you use the **SAVE** command, Logo will type a message telling you that a file with that name already exists. This keeps you from accidentally overwriting a valuable file. At this point you can either save the procedures in a new file (**NEWSQUARES**, for example) or enter

ERASEFILE "SQUAREFILE

to erase the old file and then enter

SAVE "SQUAREFILE

to save the updated version. It is safest to create a new file before deleting an old one, so that you don't risk losing everything in the event of a power failure while Logo is saving your procedures.

If you find that you no longer want a procedure in your Logo workspace (the procedure **SQUARE**, for example), enter

ERASE "SQUARE

Remember that the commands **SAVE, LOAD, CATA-LOG**, and **ERASEFILE** work with collections of procedure definitions on your file diskette and that **TO** and **ERASE** work with specific procedures in the Apple's workspace.

At this point you might want to experiment with the creation of some new procedures. For example, I always have to look up the number to use with **SETPC** to change the turtle's pen to a specific color. Since

Logo already has a **PENERASE** command, why not create the commands **PENWHITE**, **PENBLUE**, **PENORANGE**, and so forth, to change the pen to the named color? Practice saving your extensions of Logo on the file diskette, erasing them from the workspace, and then bringing them back into your workspace from the file diskette.

Procedures of One Variable

We have a procedure that draws a 50-unit square, but suppose that you want to define a procedure that lets you draw a square of any size. In our previous procedure we had the turtle move forward by a fixed number of units each time. To make a procedure that draws a square of any size, we need to find a way to have the turtle move forward by some number of units that won't be specified until we use the procedure. Instead of using **FORWARD 50**, we need to replace the 50 with a *variable* that is specified when **SQUARE** is used.

In Logo, words can be used as names under which information is stored. This means, for example, that we can use a word such as **SIZE** to contain the number of steps we want for each side of the **SQUARE**. **SIZE** is the name of the variable, and the thing that **SIZE** contains would be the length of each side.

Since variables are a very important part of Logo, we will spend a little more time discussing them before building our new **SQUARE** procedure. Logo variables can contain any of three types of information: numbers, words, and lists. To see how variables work, let's do an experiment. Enter

TEXTSCREEN

since we will be using only text for the time being.

To make a Logo variable contain something, we use the **MAKE** command. We can make the variable **TEST** contain the number 4 by entering

MAKE "TEST 4

To see that the word **TEST** contains the number 4, we can print the thing contained in **TEST** on the screen by entering

PRINT THING "TEST

The number 4 appears on the screen as soon as you press RETURN.

Using **MAKE** and **PRINT** in this way, you will see that a Logo variable can hold words and lists as well as numbers. (Remember that words need a quotation mark at the beginning and that lists are enclosed in square brackets.)

It is quite common to want to use the thing associated with a variable, and typing **THING** each time can be cumbersome. To make life easier, Logo has a short form for **THING**. To see how it works, enter the following:

MAKE "TEST 64
PRINT :TEST

The number 64 will appear on the screen, showing that the short form :TEST is equivalent to **THING** "TEST.

We are now ready to build our new (SQUARE) procedure. We will use the word **SIZE** to denote the length of our square's side. To define the new procedure, first erase any old copy that might be in the workspace. (To see the names of any procedures you have created, you can use the command **POTS** to Print Out TitleS of the procedures on the screen.) Next, enter

TO SQUARE :SIZE
REPEAT 4 [FORWARD :SIZE RIGHT 90]
END

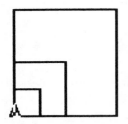

Notice that the thing associated with SIZE appears in two places—in the first line and after the word FORWARD. Now enter

SQUARE 20
SQUARE 40
SQUARE 80

to see three squares drawn on the screen.

Notice that each number you entered is passed by the SQUARE procedure to the FORWARD command inside this procedure. The SQUARE procedure can thus be used to create a square of any size.

Polygons and Pathways

The square is but one example of a regular polygon. One can construct regular polygons with any number of sides greater than two. Let's examine some of the simpler polygons. Enter

CLEARSCREEN
REPEAT 3 [FORWARD 50 RIGHT 120]

This puts a triangle on the screen. Next, let's create a square by entering

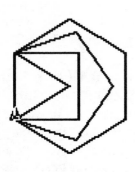

REPEAT 4 [FORWARD 50 RIGHT 90]

To see a regular pentagon, enter

REPEAT 5 [FORWARD 50 RIGHT 72]

and to draw a hexagon, enter

REPEAT 6 [FORWARD 50 RIGHT 60]

What do these four figures have in common? They are all closed paths, since the turtle always ends up exactly where it starts. They also were drawn with identical side lengths. In addition to all this, however, there is something these figures share with all simple closed paths—something that will let us create a procedure to draw any regular polygon we wish.

The Turtle's Total Trip

If you study the commands that created each polygon, you will notice that as the number of sides increases, the amount the turtle turns at each corner decreases. To draw a triangle, we turn by 120 degrees; a square results from a turn of 90 degrees; and a pentagon and hexagon use turning angles of 72 and 60 degrees, respectively.

The discovery we can make comes from looking at the total amount turned for each polygon. The following table shows the results of this calculation.

POLYGON	NUMBER OF TURNS	AMOUNT TURNED AT EACH CORNER	TOTAL AMOUNT TURNED
triangle	3	120	360
square	4	90	360
pentagon	5	72	360
hexagon	6	60	360

From this table, we see that the total amount turned in following any simple polygonal path is 360 degrees.

You can test this rule for any simple closed figure (one that does not cross over itself). In adding up the angles, you must subtract turns to the left from turns to the right, since if you turn to the right by some amount and then turn to the left by the same amount, your turns cancel each other out. Consider this hexagon. It was drawn by the following commands:

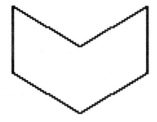

FORWARD 50 RIGHT 120
FORWARD 60 LEFT 60
FORWARD 60 RIGHT 120
FORWARD 50 RIGHT 60
FORWARD 60 RIGHT 60
FORWARD 60 RIGHT 60

If we add up all the turns to the right we get 420 degrees; if we then subtract the 60-degree turn to the left, we see that the net turning angle is 420 − 60, or 360 degrees.

The name of the rule we have found is the Turtle Total Trip Theorem. Using this rule, we can define a new procedure that draws any regular polygon. If we specify the number of sides in the polygon, then the amount turned at each corner is 360 divided by the number of sides. Logo uses the solidus (/) to indicate division. The general polygon procedure is as follows:

```
TO POLY :SIZE :SIDES
REPEAT :SIDES [FORWARD :SIZE RIGHT 360   /   :SIDES]
END
```

Let's try out this procedure for all polygons from triangles to nonagons (nine sides). Enter

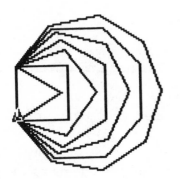

```
CLEARSCREEN
POLY 40 3
POLY 40 4
POLY 40 5
POLY 40 6
POLY 40 7
POLY 40 8
POLY 40 9
```

Fig. 4.6

As you can see, the **POLY** procedure works perfectly.

The total trip theorem is one of the most significant rules you will learn in this book. We will be exploring its ramifications in the chapters that follow.

V.

Tiles and Tessellations

Of all the constraints on nature, the most far-reaching are imposed by space. For space itself has a structure that influences the shape of every existing thing.

(from Patterns in Nature, **Peter Stevens)**

We are surrounded by patterns that fill two-dimensional space. Some of these patterns, such as murals and stained-glass windows, are finished works of art that are whole in themselves and are not designed to be replicated as repeated patterns. Other figures, such as those found on wallpaper, for example, consist of a basic motif that is designed to be repeated as many times as is necessary to cover a surface.

The design of motifs that can be replicated to fill two-dimensional space is an interesting topic for study. The basic motif is chosen for its visually attractive elements; when it is repeated in both horizontal and vertical directions, it should create an overall pattern that is also visually pleasing.

Compared to other replicating patterns, wallpaper designs are fairly unconstrained. One can start with almost any simple figure and repeat it at points on a regular grid to form an overall pattern. To see how a wallpaper design might be made, let's choose a simple motif—a five-pointed star (stars are sufficiently interesting that we will study them in detail in the next chapter):

```
TO MOTIF
REPEAT 5 [FORWARD 20 RIGHT 144]
END
```

If you now enter

```
HIDETURTLE
MOTIF
```

you will see the basic pattern.

Next, let's create the procedures that allow us to replicate this pattern in a wallpaper design. To do this, we must move the turtle to the upper left edge of the screen. Then we need a procedure that uses the procedure **MOTIF**, turns the turtle to the right, moves it by some amount (the repeat distance), and turns the turtle back to its original position. If we keep using this procedure, we should get a horizontal chain of stars on the screen. See if you can create this procedure yourself. Here is one way to do it:

```
TO HORPATTERN :STEP
MOTIF
PENUP
RIGHT 90 FORWARD :STEP LEFT 90
PENDOWN
END
```

To try this out, we will remove the wraparound feature of the display screen to let the turtle move as far in each direction as it needs to. We will pick the position [– 130 75] as the starting point and draw a line of stars. Enter

```
CLEARSCREEN
WINDOW
PENUP
SETPOS [ - 130 75]
PENDOWN
REPEAT 10 [HORPATTERN 20]
```

As you can see, we now have a row of stars. To turn this into a wallpaper pattern, we need to have a procedure that moves the turtle back to the horizontal starting position and then moves it down the screen by some distance. The procedure **VERTSTEP** should do this:

```
TO VERTSTEP :STEP
PENUP
SETX  - 130
RIGHT 180 FORWARD :STEP LEFT 180
PENDOWN
END
```

[NOTE: The command **SETX** moves the turtle to the horizontal (x) position specified without changing the vertical (y) position at all. As you might imagine, there is also a corresponding command, **SETY**.]

To see how our new procedure works, enter

```
VERTSTEP 20
REPEAT 10 [HORPATTERN 20]
```

to get a new row of stars.

Finally, we can create a "wallpaper generator" to fill the screen with an array of figures generated by **MOTIF**:

```
TO WALLPAPER :XSTEP :YSTEP
PENUP
SETPOS [ - 130 75]
PENDOWN
REPEAT 10 [REPEAT 10 [HORPATTERN :XSTEP]
  VERTSTEP :YSTEP]
END
```

[NOTE: When entering long lines (such as the fifth line of the foregoing procedure) do not press RETURN until you have finished the entire entry (for example, until after you have typed :YSTEP]). Logo will automatically break the line at the edge of the screen as many times as are necessary until you complete the entry.]

To get the full benefit of WALLPAPER, enter FULLSCREEN and examine the patterns you get with WALLPAPER 17 20, WALLPAPER 10 30, and WALLPAPER 30 30.

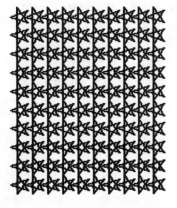

In the first of these patterns (WALLPAPER 17 20), the stars just touch each other to form a closed network pattern.

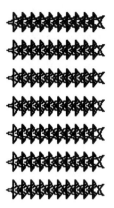

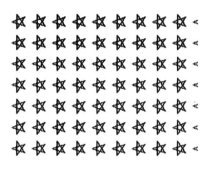

In the second pattern (WALLPAPER 10 30), the stars overlap in the horizontal direction and are spread apart vertically. This generates an interesting sawtooth pattern in the white space.

Finally, in the third pattern, we see rows of isolated stars.

Patterns made by repeating motifs can create new graphic elements by the interaction of adjacent replicas of the original motif. Each of the previous three figures was generated by the same procedure, yet the resulting patterns were quite different from one another.

Space-Filling Polygons

Next, let's explore patterns that result from the interlocking of identical figures. This is a bit more challenging than working with wallpaper designs, because we want to use figures that interlock perfectly to fill a plane without leaving any gaps. Instead of wallpaper, we will study patterns that are more reminiscent of tile floors. Patterns made from such perfectly interlocking motifs are called *tessellations*.

How many tessellating patterns are there? There is a limitless number of patterns that tessellate, just as there is a limitless number of patterns that don't tessellate. We will discover a rule that lets us find out in advance whether certain motifs can be used to tessellate a plane.

Let's start with regular polygons. In Chapter I, we mentioned that one could fill a plane with triangles, squares, and hexagons, but not with pentagons. Starting with equilateral triangles, we can see that there are any number of ways that identical triangles can be arranged to fill space. These figures show two examples.

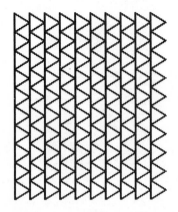

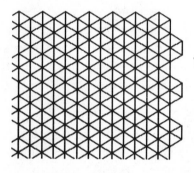

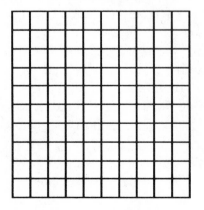

The same is true of squares.

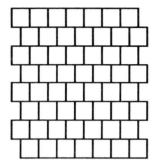

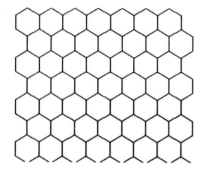

Hexagons, however, are unique. There is only one way to arrange hexagons so that they fill space.

The hexagon lies at the boundary dividing regular polygons that can tessellate (those with three, four, or six sides) from those that, by themselves, cannot fill a plane (those with any number of sides more than six). But what about the five-sided pentagon? We saw in Chapter I that it couldn't be used to tile a plane. We will show why soon.

What happens if we try to tessellate a plane with a polygon that has more than six sides? Let's try using an octagon and see what we get. To generate an octagon, we can use the **POLY** procedure defined in Chapter IV. If this procedure is not presently in your Logo workspace, you should retrieve it from the diskette or create a new copy. Next, we need to modify **MOTIF** to draw an octagon. First enter

ERASE ''MOTIF

and then enter the procedure

TO MOTIF
POLY 20 8
END

If you enter

CLEARSCREEN
MOTIF

you will see an octagon on the screen.

To see an attempt to tessellate a plane with octagons, enter

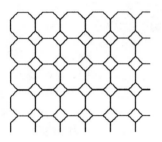

CLEARSCREEN
WALLPAPER 48 48

The resulting pattern shows that space can be filled with an interlocking arrangement of octagons and squares. Although polygons with more than six sides can't fill space by themselves, they can be part of a space-filling pattern that uses other polygons.

To see a major property of all tessellating figures, let's start by looking at a node where three hexagons join. The turtle is at the point of interest.

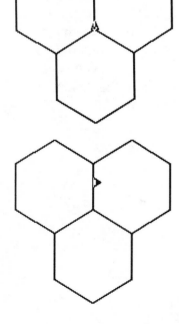

Suppose that we place the turtle at some location away from this point and face it to the right.

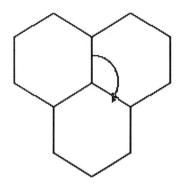

If we were to draw any closed figure around the node from this starting point, the turtle would have to turn by 360 degrees. We know this result from the Turtle Total Trip Theorem. Suppose that we move along an arc in the first hexagon. (The interior angle of a hexagon is 120 degrees.)

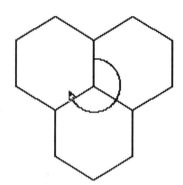

If we repeat this movement for the second and third hexagons, we turn an additional 240 degrees, giving us 360 degrees overall.

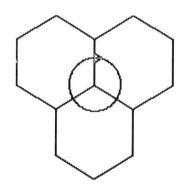

From this example, we can see that, for polygons to tessellate, the sum of the interior angles measured around each node where three or more polygons meet must be 360 degrees.

Notice that the angle of concern is different from the one by which the turtle turns when it draws the polygon in the first place. To draw an angle for an equilateral triangle, for example, the turtle turns by 120 degrees.

The interior angle is the amount by which the turtle would then have to turn to be pointing back along the original direction. In our example this is 60 degrees.

The sum of the interior and exterior angles is always 180 degrees for any angle. Using this information, we can determine which polygons tessellate and which do not. For equilateral triangles, the interior angle is 60 degrees. If we divide this into 360 degrees, we see that exactly six such triangles can meet at a node and exactly fill a two-dimensional space. Thus, as we already know, we can make a tessellating pattern from triangles.

For squares, the interior angle is 90 degrees. Four squares meet at a corner to give exactly 360 degrees. For hexagons, the interior angle is 120 degrees, thus allowing exactly three hexagons to meet at a corner.

But what about the pentagon? To draw a regular pentagon, the turtle must turn by 72 degrees at each corner. This yields an interior angle of 180 − 72, or 108 degrees. If we place three pentagons together, the total combined angle is 324 degrees—not enough to fill space. Yet four pentagons give 432 degrees—far too much. This is why it is impossible to tessellate a plane with regular pentagonal tiles.

We can use the same rules when analyzing tessellations that use combinations of polygons, such as the combination of octagons and squares. In that case, the octagons have interior angles of 180 − 45, or 135 degrees. Two octagons meet to give a combined angle of 270 degrees. The 90-degree corner of a square brings us exactly to the desired value of 360 degrees, thus confirming what we already knew from experiment.

Thus the total trip theorem has led us to another valuable rule—one that governs all tessellating figures.

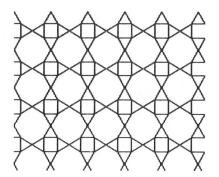

You should experiment with mixtures of regular polygons to find other combinations that produce tessellations. For example, you might want to analyze the different types of nodes in the tessellating figure shown here.

Other Space-Filling Figures

Tessellating figures are in no way limited to regular polygons. The chevron-shaped figure we drew in the previous chapter tessellates quite nicely. To see this, erase MOTIF and replace it with the procedure

```
TO MOTIF
FORWARD 50 RIGHT 120
FORWARD 60 LEFT 60
FORWARD 60 RIGHT 120
FORWARD 50 RIGHT 60
FORWARD 60 RIGHT 60
FORWARD 60 RIGHT 60
END
```

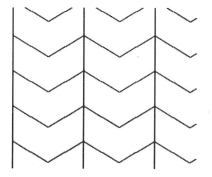

and enter

```
CLEARSCREEN
WALLPAPER 104 50
```

You can spend many hours finding hundreds upon hundreds of tessellating shapes. If you are familiar with the artwork of M. C. Escher, you have no doubt noticed that he has created numerous tessellating patterns from birds, fish, salamanders, and the like.

Although some patterns cannot be used to fill space, there is no limit to the creation of tessellating patterns once you know the rules.

VI.

Stars and Primes

We had the sky, up there, all speckled with stars, and we used to lay on our backs and look up at them and discuss about whether they was made, or only just happened.

(**from** Huckleberry Finn, **Mark Twain**)

Complex Polygons

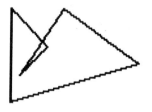

The Turtle Total Trip Theorem applies to simple polygons—those polygons whose lines don't cross over each other. But this type of polygon is just one of a larger family of figures made from straight lines. Technically, any closed figure made from straight lines is a polygon. A complex polygon (such as that shown) obeys another form of the total trip theorem, which we will develop later in this chapter.

One type of complex polygon that is quite beautiful is the star. (We saw one example of a star in the previous chapter.) For example, if you enter

CLEARSCREEN
REPEAT 5 [FORWARD 50 RIGHT 144]

you will have a five-pointed star on the screen.

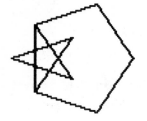

Next, let's create another five-sided figure—a regular pentagon. Enter

REPEAT 5 [FORWARD 50 RIGHT 72]

The only difference in the instructions that drew these figures is that we turned 144 degrees after drawing each line on the star and 72 degrees after drawing each line on the pentagon. To draw a star, we doubled the angle we used to draw a pentagon. If we were to write the instructions for drawing a pentagon this way:

REPEAT 5 [FORWARD 50 RIGHT (360 / 5)]

then we would write the instructions for a five-pointed star this way:

REPEAT 5 [FORWARD 50 RIGHT (360 * 2 / 5)]

[NOTE: Logo uses the asterisk (*) to denote multiplication.]

Clear the screen and use the previous two commands to see how they work.

Let's see if the key to making a star from any simple polygon involves simply doubling the turning angle. Enter

CLEARSCREEN
REPEAT 6 [FORWARD 50 RIGHT (360 / 6)]

to draw a hexagon. Then enter the following command to see if it produces a six-pointed star:

REPEAT 6 [FORWARD 50 RIGHT (360 * 2 / 6)]

Instead of drawing a star, the second instruction drew a triangle.

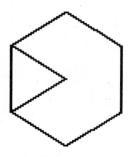

Stars and Relatively Prime Numbers

·

To find out which turning angles produce stars and which do not, it would be useful to have a procedure that lets us try patterns out quickly. The procedure we seek is similar to POLY, except that it has a multiplier that needs to be specified. Here is one way to write this procedure:

```
TO STAR :MULT :SIDES
REPEAT :SIDES [FORWARD 50 RIGHT (360 * :MULT /
  :SIDES)]
END
```

Test this procedure by entering

```
CLEARSCREEN
STAR 1 5
```

This should draw a simple regular pentagon on the screen. If you then enter

```
STAR 2 5
```

you should see a five-pointed star as well.

To see why some combinations of multipliers and sides produce stars while others do not, let's examine some patterns based on nine-sided polygons. Enter

```
CLEARSCREEN
PENUP
SETPOS [ −25 −25]
PENDOWN
STAR 1 9
```

to draw a simple nonagon. Then enter

```
STAR 2 9
```

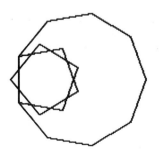

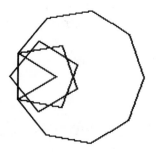

The last command generated a nine-pointed star. Next, let's change the multiplier to 3 and see what happens:

STAR 3 9

This last command generated a triangle.

To organize our search for star-producing combinations of multipliers and sides, we can make a table with this heading:

STAR TABLE

MULTIPLIER	SIDES	STAR? (YES OR NO)

In the first two columns, we will put the values we try for various multipliers and numbers of sides; then we will note what kind of figure each combination produces.

In creating these patterns, we need to know the limit for trial values of the multiplier. Suppose that we choose a multiplier whose value is the same as the number of sides in the polygon. In this case the turtle would turn 360 degrees at the end of each line, and the figure would never close. Thus we see that we must limit our multiplier to a value less than the number of sides.

For our purposes, we won't have to use multipliers whose value is greater than half the number of sides. To see why, let's experiment with various seven-sided polygons. To keep the screen uncluttered, you might wish to clear the screen after generating each of the figures.

STAR 1 7
STAR 2 7
STAR 3 7
STAR 4 7
STAR 5 7
STAR 6 7

If we look carefully at the six polygons we just drew, we can see that **STAR 6 7** produced a mirror image of the regular heptagon drawn by **STAR 1 7**.

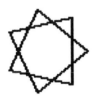

Other mirror images can be seen in the figures drawn by **STAR 2 7** and **STAR 5 7** and in those drawn by **STAR 3 7** and **STAR 4 7**. As we use multipliers greater than half the number of sides, we generate mirror images of the preceding patterns in reverse order until we once again create the simple regular polygon.

Since no new patterns are generated when we use numbers larger than half the number of sides, this simplifies our task in filling out the star table. In filling out your copy of the table, remember that our goal is the production of stars with the same number of points as the number of drawn sides. There were two such stars for the heptagon—one with a multiplier of 2 and another with a multiplier of 3.

The following table shows the results for polygons with up to 11 sides:

STAR TABLE

MULTIPLIER	SIDES	STAR? (YES OR NO)
2	4	NO
2	5	YES
2	6	NO
3	6	NO
2	7	YES
3	7	YES
2	8	NO
3	8	YES
4	8	NO
2	9	YES
3	9	NO
4	9	YES
2	10	NO
3	10	YES
4	10	NO (5-pointed)
5	10	NO
2	11	YES
3	11	YES
4	11	YES
5	11	YES

We did not include a multiplier of 1 in the table because we already know that we will get a simple polygon with that value.

As we look at this table, we see many yeses and many noes. Let's look more closely to see if there is a pattern to these results. First let's see if there are any polygons for which all multipliers (greater than 1) give a star. We can see that when the number of sides is equal to 5, 7, or 11, all values of multipliers produce stars! The numbers 5, 7, and 11 are prime numbers—

numbers that cannot be formed by the multiplication of two whole numbers, both of which must be greater than 1. The number 6 is not a prime number, since 6 is 2 * 3; the numbers 2 and 3 are the factors of 6. The number 7, however, cannot be written as the product of two whole numbers, so it is a prime number.

So far, we have discovered that polygons whose number of sides equals a prime number can be turned into stars for any multiplier other than 1 or number of sides less 1. But what about numbers like 8? When we look at polygons with eight sides, we find that some multipliers give stars and others don't. Let's look at this more closely. With eight-sided polygons, multipliers of 2 or 4 don't produce stars, but a multiplier of 3 does. Now it so happens that both 2 and 4 are factors of 8. We do get a star when we use 3, but 3 is not a factor of 8. When we consider nine-sided polygons, we see the same sort of thing. In any particular case, if the multiplier and the number of sides have a common factor, we will not get a star with the same number of points as drawn sides. We can thus create a rule for stars:

A polygon with *S* sides can be turned into a star with *S* points by increasing each turning angle by *M* times, when *M* is a whole number that shares no factors with *S*.

Before concluding this chapter, we should revisit the total trip theorem. For simple closed figures, the turtle always turns a total of 360 degrees. For the five-pointed star (STAR 2 5), the total turning angle was 720 degrees (2 * 360). For the two seven-pointed stars, the turning angles were 720 degrees and 1080 degrees (3 * 360), respectively. Notice that as the total turning angle increases, the lines of the star move closer to the center of the figure.

We can now rephrase the total trip theorem to cover any polygon:

For any closed figure, the total turning angle will be N * 360, where N is an integer greater than or equal to 1.

VII.

Procedures Using Procedures

To see a world in a grain of sand
And heaven in a wild flower,
Hold infinity in the palm of your hand
And eternity in an hour.

(from Auguries of Innocence,
William Blake)

Thus far we have learned, among other things, how to extend Logo by the creation of procedures. In this chapter we will explore, among other things, the ability of procedures to use other procedures.

To start with a simple example, suppose that we want to draw a five-pointed star. We can do this using the **STAR** procedure described in the previous chapter. After making certain that the procedure is in the Logo workspace, enter

```
CLEARSCREEN
STAR 2 5
```

Now suppose that we want to draw this same star each time we use another word—PENTAGRAM, for example. To do that we can create the procedure

```
TO PENTAGRAM
STAR 2 5
END
```

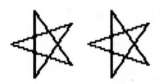

If we now relocate the turtle by entering

PENUP SETPOS [60 0] PENDOWN

and enter

PENTAGRAM

we will see a second identical star on the screen.

The procedure **PENTAGRAM** uses the procedure **STAR**. One of Logo's features is that procedures can use each other and can even pass variables to each other. For example, suppose you grew tired of entering the word **STAR** each time and wanted to be able to just enter a single letter, S. This procedure will accomplish this task for you:

```
TO S :MULT :SIDES
STAR :MULT :SIDES
END
```

Now you can create a star by using either **S** or **STAR**. In other words, **S** 7 15 generates the same figure as **STAR** 7 15, because both commands ultimately use the same **STAR** procedure.

As you experiment some more with this idea, try creating a procedure that uses **STAR** but reverses the order of the inputs. This procedure—let's call it T— has the property that T 14 3 generates the same figure as **STAR** 3 14.

Windmills and Flower Blossoms

We are now in a position to develop some new procedures that use some old procedures (such as **POLY**) to explore some aspects of rotational symmetry. If you have not already done so, you should make sure that **POLY** is in your Logo workspace.

Some very nice patterns can be made by taking a simple object and repeating it at equal angles around the center of the screen. Because of the flowerlike patterns that often result, we will call the procedure that does this FLOWER.

FLOWER needs two pieces of information to do its job. First, it needs to know how many times to repeat the pattern around the center of the screen, and then it needs a list of instructions for generating the pattern to be repeated. We already know that in a procedure like STAR, the command STAR 2 5 will cause the numbers 2 and 5 to be passed to the appropriate places of the procedure definition so they can be used. Logo variables can be numbers, words, or lists. If we want to pass a series of Logo instructions to a procedure, the easiest way is to pass them as a list. This means that we would bundle the instructions together and enclose them in square brackets. (The Logo command RE-PEAT operates this way.) To draw eight pentagons around the screen, we might enter FLOWER 8 [POLY 40 5]. The value of the first variable is the number 8 and the value of the second variable is a list containing the instructions POLY 40 5.

Once an instruction list is passed to a procedure, we need to be able to instruct Logo to run the instructions. After all, the elements in the list might be just words, they might be the names of variables, or, as in this case, they might be a sequence of Logo commands. To run a list containing Logo commands, we use the RUN command. The command RUN is always followed by a list containing a series of instructions made of Logo commands and procedures.

The FLOWER procedure uses RUN in the following way:

```
TO FLOWER :SIDES :INSTRUCTIONLIST
REPEAT :SIDES [RUN :INSTRUCTIONLIST RIGHT
   360 / :SIDES]
END
```

[NOTE: Remember that our choice of variable names is for our own convenience in remembering what they should contain. We could just as easily have created the procedure as FLOWER :GEORGE :FREDDY.]

Before using this new procedure, it is interesting to compare FLOWER with a similar procedure, POLY:

```
TO POLY :SIZE :SIDES
REPEAT :SIDES [FORWARD :SIZE RIGHT 360/:SIDES]
END
```

The only difference between FLOWER and POLY is that POLY uses the single command FORWARD before turning, whereas FLOWER is set up to use any number of commands before turning. To examine this further, enter

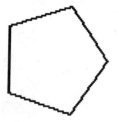

```
CLEARSCREEN
FLOWER 5 [FORWARD 50]
```

By letting FLOWER use the command FORWARD 50, we drew the same pentagon we would have drawn with POLY 50 5.

FLOWER is much more general than POLY, however, since we can use any combination of commands in place of FORWARD. As an example, let's try the following:

```
CLEARSCREEN
FLOWER 5 [FORWARD 30 REPEAT 5 [FORWARD 20
   RIGHT 144] ]
```

This procedure generated a pattern of five stars on the corners of a pentagon.

We should make note of the fact that FLOWER has thus far produced closed figures. Is this always the case? We can show that it is not by example:

CLEARSCREEN
FLOWER 5 [FORWARD 20 LEFT 30]

The reason this figure is not closed is that the turtle did not turn a net multiple of 360 degrees in generating the figure. FLOWER will always create closed figures so long as the procedures and commands in INSTRUC-TIONLIST leave the turtle pointing in the same direction it was pointing at the beginning of the commands. In other words, if the net turning in INSTRUCTION-LIST is zero or a multiple of 360 degrees, FLOWER will always generate a closed figure. For example, enter

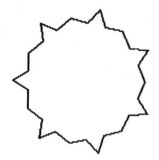

CLEARSCREEN
FLOWER 7 [FORWARD 20 LEFT 60 FORWARD 20
    RIGHT 120 FORWARD 20 LEFT 60 FORWARD 20]

The commands FORWARD 20 LEFT 60 FORWARD 20 RIGHT 120 FORWARD 20 LEFT 60 FORWARD 20 have a net turning angle of zero, and the resulting figure is closed.

Aside from generating some interesting patterns, FLOWER can let us explore some aspects of rotational symmetry. For example, suppose that we create a pentagon by using

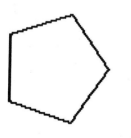

CLEARSCREEN
POLY 50 5

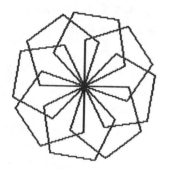

This figure has fivefold rotational symmetry. If we now create a flower pattern from this pentagon by entering

FLOWER 8 [POLY 50 5]

we have generated a new figure that has eightfold rotational symmetry.

    In other words, **FLOWER** creates a figure whose rotational symmetry is determined by the number of rotations made by **FLOWER**, not by the symmetry of the repeated pattern used by **FLOWER**.

    Each of the following commands generates a figure with eightfold symmetry, even though the individual elements that are repeated have threefold, fourfold, fivefold, or sixfold rotational symmetry. (You may wish to clear the screen before drawing each of these patterns.)

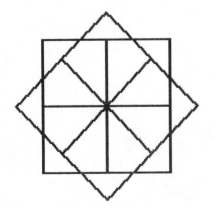

FLOWER 8 [POLY 50 3]

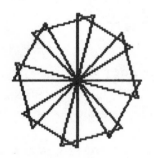

FLOWER 8 [POLY 50 4]

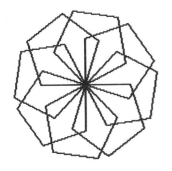

FLOWER 8 [POLY 50 5]

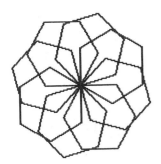

FLOWER 8 [POLY 40 6]

This shows that a pattern of one symmetry can be used as the building block of a pattern with any other symmetry. It is interesting to note that there is no limit to how far this can go. For example, suppose that we created a triangle by using

POLY 40 3

This figure has threefold symmetry. Next let's use FLOWER with this pattern to generate a figure with eightfold symmetry:

FLOWER 8 [POLY 40 3]

Next we will use FLOWER to repeat this pattern to generate a figure with fivefold symmetry. We do this by having FLOWER use itself. The act of having a procedure use itself is called *recursion*. Because vari-

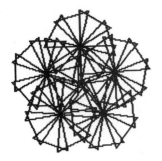

able names in Logo are locally defined within each procedure each time it is used, a procedure can use itself or any other procedures with the same variable names without confusion. Recursion will be covered in far greater detail in a later chapter. Meanwhile, to see that it works, enter

CLEARSCREEN
FLOWER 5 [FORWARD 40 [FLOWER 8 [POLY 40 3]
  BACK 40]]

Notice that we used **FORWARD** and **BACK** to move our eightfold pattern off center. The resulting flower (is it an apple blossom?) has fivefold symmetry and is made from elements with eightfold symmetry that are made from elements with threefold symmetry. The symmetry of the overall figure is determined by the last symmetry operation performed.

VIII.

Angles, Squares, and Squirals

What comes out of all this is that a spiral is a figure that retains its shape (i.e., proportion) as it grows in one dimension by addition at the open end. You see, there are no truly static spirals.

(from Mind and Nature,
Gregory Bateson)

Thus far, we have explored graphic procedures that produce static images. In looking at their finished form, there is no clue to the process that created them. In this chapter, we will explore some classes of geometric figures that are formed by a sequential growth process. Generally, this means that we will be dealing with a set of commands that are repeated to form the object. By increasing the size of the lines drawn with each repetition of the command sequence, an object is caused to grow on the display screen. Logo provides us with several ways to perform this task. Central to each of them is the concept of a counter.

Counters

Suppose that we want to create a procedure that types out the sequence of numbers 0, 1, 2, 3, . . . How would we do this? We could use a variable to store the number we are counting, but we need to know how to have Logo change this number each time it is used. One way to make a counter is to place the starting number in a variable (using the **MAKE** command) and then make the new value of the variable by adding one to the old value. For example, consider the following counter procedure:

```
TO COUNTER1 :VALUE
PRINT :VALUE
MAKE "VALUE :VALUE + 1
COUNTER1 :VALUE
END
```

If you now try this procedure by entering

```
COUNTER1 0
```

your screen will display a column of numbers starting from 0 and continuing upward in increments of one. We did not provide any way for COUNTER1 to stop. This procedure lets us be like the sorcerer's apprentice in Walt Disney's *Fantasia*, who started having a broom to do his chores for him but couldn't stop it when it got out of control. Fortunately, we can stop the execution of any Logo activity very easily. To stop the counter, hold down the key marked CTRL and press the G key. Logo will then let you know that you stopped a procedure and will return control of the computer to you.

The procedure COUNTER1 is but one of many ways of making a counter. There is a shorter way that might seem to be a little harder to understand. Enter the procedure

```
TO COUNTER2 :VALUE
PRINT :VALUE
COUNTER2 :VALUE + 1
END
```

If you now enter COUNTER2 0, you will see that it behaves similarly to COUNTER1. The secret to COUNTER2 is the third line. When this procedure uses itself again, the number that is passed to the next use of **VALUE** is the old value plus one. We will see more examples of this type of parameter passing in a later chapter. For our purposes, the explicit use of the **MAKE** command is perhaps easier to understand.

When making a counter, it is often a good idea to have it stop when it reaches a preset limit. What we want is to have the procedure use itself over and over again, so long as the number counted is not greater than the limit. Logo provides ways to test for certain conditions and to do something on the basis of the test results. The technique we will explore uses the **IF** command. Structurally, this command takes the form (in Apple Logo):

IF *predicate list*

A Logo predicate is a special word or expression that is either true or false. Suppose that we want to test if a number stored in the variable **VALUE** is greater than 100. In Apple Logo we would write

IF :VALUE $>$ 100 *list*

[NOTE: The symbols $<$, $=$, and $>$ are used to compare two numbers to see if the first is less than, equal to, or greater than the second, respectively.]

After the predicate, the Logo **IF** command needs a list of commands to be executed in the event that the predicate is true. The list can be as short as one command, or it can be several commands long. In any case, the list (as all Logo lists) must be enclosed in square brackets. If the tested predicate is not true, the list will be ignored and Logo will proceed to the next line in the procedure. For our counter application, we want the procedure to stop execution when the predicate is true. The Logo command that accomplishes this is **STOP**. The entire **IF** statement looks like this:

IF :VALUE $>$ 100 [STOP]

When Logo encounters STOP in a procedure, it checks to see if there is any unfinished business in any previous procedures and then returns to the command level.

To see how this works, modify COUNTER1 to make it into COUNTER3, as follows:

```
TO COUNTER3 :VALUE :LIMIT
IF :VALUE > :LIMIT [STOP]
PRINT :VALUE
MAKE "VALUE :VALUE + 1
COUNTER3 :VALUE :LIMIT
END
```

If you then enter

```
COUNTER3 0 50
```

you will see a list of the numbers from 0 to 50. As soon as :VALUE exceeded 50, it failed the test in the IF command, and the procedure stopped. COUNTER3 was used 51 separate times. Since there was nothing left to do in the previous uses of COUNTER3, Logo returned to the command level.

Another method for making a counter involves the use of the REPEAT command. This is illustrated in the procedure COUNTER4:

```
TO COUNTER4 :VALUE :LIMIT
REPEAT (:LIMIT − :VALUE) [PRINT :VALUE MAKE
   "VALUE :VALUE + 1]
END
```

[NOTE: Normal parentheses can be used freely to group mathematical operations. This makes the operations easier to read and avoids any possibility of Logo misinterpreting them.]

The COUNTER4 procedure repeats the counter sequence by an amount given by the difference between the limit and the starting value. Since this is calculated at the very beginning of the procedure, the fact that the contents of **VALUE** is changed later does not affect the operation of this procedure.

If you now enter

COUNTER4 0 50

you will get something slightly different from the result you got with **COUNTER3**. In fact, the counter will stop at 49, since this is the fiftieth number it counted (0 was the first). You should be able to modify **COUNTER4** so it will always produce results identical to those of **COUNTER3**.

In the remainder of this chapter, we will explore ways counters can be used to assist in the creation of growing patterns.

Growing Squares

Using the counter concept, we can let Logo generate figures by a process of growth. For example, suppose that we create a procedure that generates a square:

```
TO SQUARE :SIZE
REPEAT 4 [FORWARD :SIZE RIGHT 90]
END
```

We can use this procedure inside another procedure that will generate a growing square:

```
TO GROWSQUARE :LIMIT
MAKE "SIZE 0
REPEAT :LIMIT [SQUARE :SIZE MAKE "SIZE :SIZE + 1]
END
```

If you now enter the commands

```
CLEARSCREEN
GROWSQUARE 60
```

you will see a solid square grow from a dot at the center of the screen to its final size.

If we want to make a growing open square (rather than an enlarging solid square), we need to erase each square after we draw it and then draw the next larger square. You should be able to modify GROWSQUARE to make this work. An alternative form of this type of growth is illustrated as follows for a five-pointed star:

```
TO STAR :SIZE
REPEAT 5 [FORWARD :SIZE RIGHT 144]
END
```

```
TO GROWSTAR :SIZE :LIMIT
PENDOWN STAR :SIZE
IF :SIZE > :LIMIT [STOP]
WAIT 30
PENERASE STAR :SIZE
MAKE "SIZE :SIZE + 1
GROWSTAR :SIZE :LIMIT
END
```

If you then enter

```
CLEARSCREEN
GROWSTAR 5 60
```

you will see a 5-unit star grow into a 60-unit star. The WAIT command causes the execution of the procedure to wait for thirty-sixtieths of a second before proceeding. This makes the successive stars easier to see.

Squirals

Even though you could see the growth process of the square and star, there is still no way you could have deduced this process by looking at the final figures.

Living things sometimes leave traces of their growth patterns that can be studied without watching the object grow. Seasonal cycles, for example, produce a series of concentric rings in trees. By counting the rings, one can deduce the age of the tree. A more common growth pattern, found in both plants and animals, is the spiral. The effect of spirals on the eye is so strong that they almost appear to be in motion. The curved spirals seen in snail shells, for example, are so important that we will devote a chapter to them later. The remainder of this chapter is devoted to an examination of spirals made with straight lines. These spirals are called *squirals* (square spirals).

To start, let's examine a spiral made from straight lines and square (90-degree) corners. To draw a square, we draw the same length line after each turn of 90 degrees. To draw a square spiral, we need to increase the length of each side over its previous value. Clearly, we can use a counter to do this. The following procedure will allow us to experiment with squirals containing various turning angles. The increment by which each side grows is chosen to be 2, although you may want to change this value as you experiment.

To create the **SQUIRAL** procedure, enter

```
TO SQUIRAL :ANGLE
MAKE "SIDE 0
REPEAT 100 [FORWARD :SIDE RIGHT :ANGLE MAKE
   "SIDE :SIDE + 2]
END
```

Then enter

```
WINDOW
CLEARSCREEN
SQUIRAL 90
```

This will generate a square squiral pattern on the display screen.

On examination, we can see the close relation of this figure to the square. Next, suppose that we were to use an angle close to 90 degrees—89 degrees, for example. Before trying this angle, you should try to visualize the result in your mind. Will the change be small or large? Once you have made your decision, enter

CLEARSCREEN
SQUIRAL 89

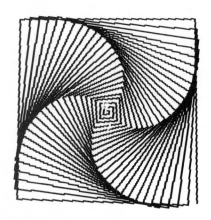

This figure looks quite different from that generated by SQUIRAL 90. Why is this?

As the figure for SQUIRAL 89 is drawn, each turning angle differs from that for a square by only one degree. But the impact of this difference is cumulative as far as the overall figure is concerned. By the time the turtle has made one circuit around the path, the difference is 4 degrees. By the time the procedure stops, the turning angle is 100 degrees in variance from its value for the truly square squiral.

One of the attractions of this figure is the four arching branches twisting to the left. These branches are formed as an interference pattern of corners that bump into each other because of the angular mismatch (compared to a square). Such interferences, called moiré patterns, are quite common. You can see moiré patterns by holding two window screens together and rotating one of them slightly with respect to the other. When the screens are adjusted so that there is no interference pattern, the screens are perfectly aligned.

We can see a similar effect with squirals. For example, if we enter

CLEARSCREEN
SQUIRAL 91

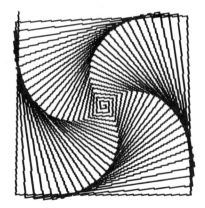

we will generate a squiral pattern that has arms branching off to the right.

Whenever we see interferences of this sort, it is a clue that we are close to a regular pattern whose alignment of sides creates no interference. If the squirals arch to the left, the angle is too small; if they arch to the right, the angle is too large.

How many squirals are there with no interference patterns? The following figures show examples of squiral patterns based on the pentagon. (You will want to clear the screen before drawing each squiral.)

SQUIRAL 70

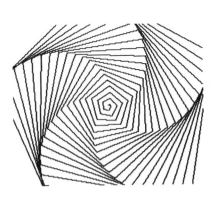

SQUIRAL 71

SQUIRAL 72

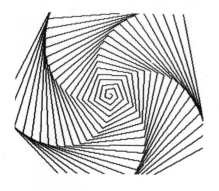

SQUIRAL 73

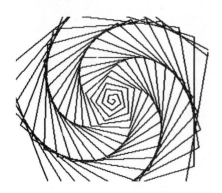

SQUIRAL 74

We can see the spiral arms in all patterns except SQUIRAL 72. The 72-degree angle is that associated with a regular pentagon. Notice that the curvature of the spiral arms is greater as you move farther away from 72 degrees in either direction.

The next set of figures explores squirals in the vicinity of 120 degrees:

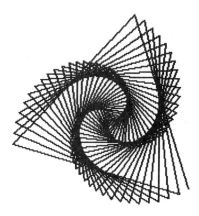

SQUIRAL 118

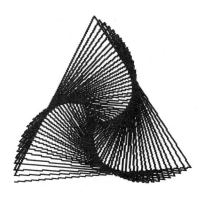

SQUIRAL 119

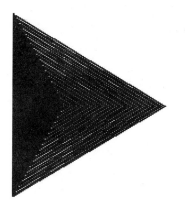

SQUIRAL 120

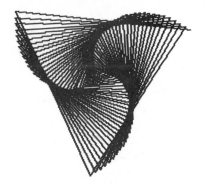

SQUIRAL 121

SQUIRAL 122

Squiral patterns need not be based on simple polygons. For example, an attractive set of figures occurs in the vicinity of 144 degrees:

SQUIRAL 142

SQUIRAL 143

SQUIRAL 144

SQUIRAL 145

SQUIRAL 146

As you experiment with the **SQUIRAL** procedure, you will find many interesting patterns. Each of these patterns reflects the process of growth by which it was created.

You see, there are no truly static spirals.

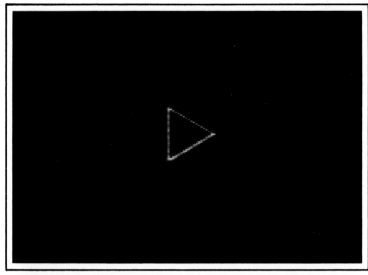

Fig. A. This sequence illustrates an interesting observation. An object with one symmetry can be used to create patterns with any other symmetry. For example, this figure shows a triangle with a simple threefold rotational axis.

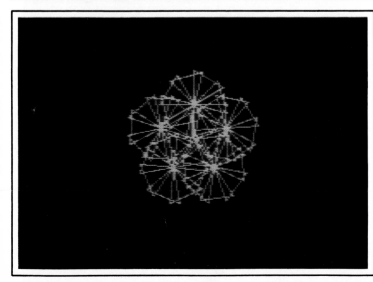

Fig. B. If the triangle is now drawn at eight equal angular increments around the origin, the resulting figure has eightfold rotational symmetry.

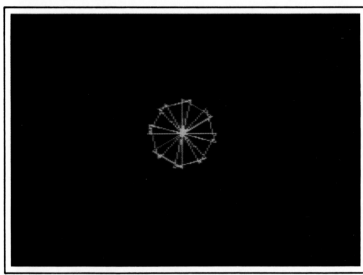

Fig. C. If this eightfold symmetric figure is now placed at five locations around the origin, the result is a flower blossom with fivefold rotational symmetry. If one looks at this figure carefully, one can still see the threefold and eightfold building blocks.

Fig. D. There are limitations to the shapes that can be used to tile a plane. While regular polygons with three, four, or six sides can be used as tiles, regular pentagons leave diamond-shaped gaps no matter how carefully they are fitted together.

Fig. E. Star polygons are closely related to their simple counterparts. By increasing the turning angle of a simple polygon by integer multiples, one gets stars sometimes but not always. The underlying selection rule for predicting the occurrence of stars is based on the properties of prime numbers.

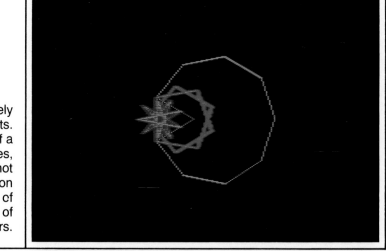

Fig. F. Binary trees convey a sense of serenity in their simplicity and yet retain the dynamic force of continued growth. This growth is reflected in the Logo procedures that generate these patterns in the form of recursion.

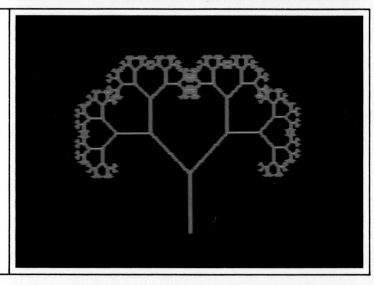

IX.

Arcs, Circles, and Spirals

Whether the symbol of the circle appears in primitive sun worship or modern religion, in myths or dreams, in the mandalas drawn by the Tibetan monks, in the ground plans of cities, or in the spherical concepts of early astronomers, it always points to the single most vital aspect of life—its ultimate wholeness.

(from Man and His Symbols, **Carl Jung)**

Thus far, our figures have been made from straight line segments. As pretty as some of these figures are, there are many other figures to be explored that use curved lines.

Central to curved figures is the shape of the circle. Given that Logo can move forward and can turn (but cannot do both simultaneously), how can we create a procedure to draw a circle?

Circles

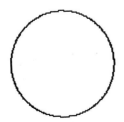

One way to create a close approximation to a circle is to draw a short line segment, turn a little, and repeat this process until the figure is closed. Using the total trip theorem, we can tell that our figure will be complete when we have turned 360 degrees.

To try this concept, enter

CLEARSCREEN
REPEAT 360 [FORWARD 1 RIGHT 1]

This figure appears to be a circle, but it is really a 360-gon. To the limit of the Apple's display resolution, however, this polygon is a close enough approximation to a circle for us to call it by that name.

To make smaller circles, we can increase the turning angle. If we turn by a greater amount, the figure will close back on itself more rapidly and thus create a smaller circle. The following procedure lets us test this concept:

```
TO CIRCLE :SIZE :ANGLE
REPEAT 360 / :ANGLE [FORWARD :SIZE RIGHT
   :ANGLE]
END
```

The reason for making the repeat factor 360 / :ANGLE is to preserve a total turning angle of 360 degrees, as required by the total trip theorem.

To test this new procedure, enter

```
CLEARSCREEN
CIRCLE 1 1
```

Our display should show the same large circle we drew before. To generate some other circles of different sizes, enter

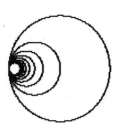

```
CIRCLE 1 2
CIRCLE 1 3
CIRCLE 1 4
CIRCLE 1 5
CIRCLE 1 6
CIRCLE 1 7
CIRCLE 1 8
CIRCLE 1 9
```

For circles of intermediate sizes, we can use other angular increments, such as 2.5, and the like.

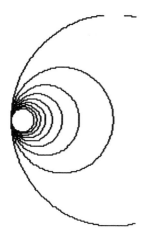

To make an even larger circle than given by CIR-CLE 1 1, we could use an angle between 0 and 1 or change the step length from 1 to some other value. For example, enter the following:

```
WINDOW
CLEARSCREEN
CIRCLE 2 1
CIRCLE 2 2
CIRCLE 2 3
CIRCLE 2 4
CIRCLE 2 5
CIRCLE 2 6
CIRCLE 2 7
CIRCLE 2 8
CIRCLE 2 9
```

Each circle in this drawing is twice as large as its counterpart in the previous figure. One can easily see the reason for this by measuring the circumference of these circles. The circumference is given by 360 / :ANGLE multiplied by the step size. For a given angle increment, doubling the step size doubles the circumference.

This observation leads to an interesting discovery: Any two circles for which the ratios of step size to angle increment are the same will have the same circumference. To test this, enter the following:

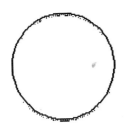

```
CLEARSCREEN
CIRCLE 1 1
SETPC 2
CIRCLE 2 2
SETPC 3
CIRCLE 3 3
SETPC 4
CIRCLE 4 4
SETPC 5
CIRCLE 5 5
```

Since each circle was drawn in a different color, it is easy to see each circle as it overlays its predecessor. Notice that, although the first few circles overlaid each other almost perfectly, the mismatch became more visible when the step size became larger. The reason for this is quite simple. We are creating circular shapes by approximation with polygons. As we increase the turning angle, we are reducing the number of sides in the polygon and thus producing a poorer approximation to a circle. As an extreme, try the following:

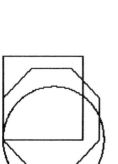

```
CLEARSCREEN
SETPC 1
CIRCLE 1 1
CIRCLE 45 45
CIRCLE 90 90
```

Each of these figures has the same circumference as the others (360 units), yet only the first resembles a circle.

Parts of Circles

Suppose that, instead of forming a complete circle, we wish to create only a portion of the circle—an arc. To do this, we need to have the turtle repeat its sequence of drawing and turning until the desired angle has been reached. For example, these two figures are both 90-degree arcs:

```
CLEARSCREEN
REPEAT 90 [FORWARD 1 RIGHT 1]
PENUP HOME PENDOWN
REPEAT 45 [FORWARD 1 RIGHT 2]
```

Even though these arcs have different sizes, they each comprise one-quarter of a circle. Arcs are useful building blocks for other figures, as we shall see in the next chapter.

Spirals

In the previous chapter, we created squirals by keeping the turning angle fixed and increasing the size of the drawn lines. By reversing this sequence, we can create some interesting spirals. To make a spiral curve, we can draw a series of fixed length lines and turn the turtle by increasing amounts at the end of each step. Using our previous experience with counters, it should not be too difficult to design a spiral procedure.

Rather than starting with such a procedure, we can create a spiral interactively by using primitive Logo commands. For example, enter

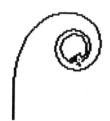

```
SHOWTURTLE
CLEARSCREEN
MAKE "ANGLE 0
REPEAT 45 [FORWARD 7 RIGHT :ANGLE MAKE
   "ANGLE :ANGLE + 1]
```

This set of instructions starts the turtle off on a gentle arc to the right that begins to circle in on itself very quickly.

Next, enter

```
REPEAT 45 [FORWARD 7 RIGHT :ANGLE MAKE
   "ANGLE :ANGLE + 1]
```

This continues to tighten the spiral. If we take an additional 90 steps (making 180 in total) by entering

```
REPEAT 90 [FORWARD 7 RIGHT :ANGLE MAKE
   "ANGLE :ANGLE + 1]
```

we will bring the turtle to the center of the circular area that is forming on the screen.

What will happen for angles greater than 180 degrees? When we started, the turtle turned first by 1 degree, then by 2 degrees, and so on. After the first four steps, the turtle had turned by only 10 degrees. Contrast this with the turning that took place at the four steps starting at 89 degrees. After these four steps, the turtle had turned more than 360 degrees. By the time we reached 180-degree increments, the turtle was simply moving back and forth over its position.

To see what happens for increments greater than 180 degrees, enter

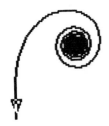

```
REPEAT 180 [FORWARD 7 RIGHT :ANGLE
    MAKE "ANGLE :ANGLE + 1]
```

At the end of 360 steps, the turtle is back at the origin, having retraced its steps. Now, however, the turtle is pointing down rather than up.

To complete the figure (and return the turtle to its home position), we need to take an additional 360 steps:

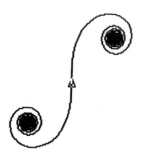

```
REPEAT 360 [FORWARD 7 RIGHT :ANGLE
    MAKE "ANGLE :ANGLE + 1]
```

This spiral figure was made by taking 720 steps. The first 360 steps created the upper right arm of the spiral, and the second 360 steps created the lower left arm.

If we were to continue repeating these same commands, we would retrace the original figure. Unlike the squiral patterns, this spiral is a closed figure. Whereas the squiral displays dynamic symmetry, the complete form of this spiral is as static and complete as a simple polygon, such as a square or a triangle.

This type of spiral is but one member of a whole family of such curves. A procedure that lets us create this and other examples of closed spirals is as follows:

```
TO CLOSESPI :SIZE :ANGLE :INCREMENT
REPEAT 720 [FORWARD :SIZE RIGHT :ANGLE
  MAKE "ANGLE :ANGLE + :INCREMENT]
END
```

This procedure lets us create figures with different angle increments and with different starting angles. Our previous spiral can be drawn by entering

```
CLEARSCREEN
CLOSESPI 7 0 1
```

Suppose that, instead of increasing the turning angle in 1-degree steps, we choose another value—for example, 7 degrees. On first thought, we might expect to get a smaller version of the existing spiral, since we have changed only the increment by which the angle is changed. To see what happens, enter

```
CLEARSCREEN
CLOSESPI 7 0 7
```

This surprising result occurs because the increment was chosen to keep us from reaching a turning angle of 180 degrees in the first arm of the spiral. As a result, the curve could not retrace itself until this condition was met.

More polygonal forms of the spiral can be made by starting with an offset angle. These three figures were made using

```
CLOSESPI 15 40 30
```

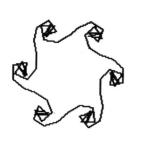

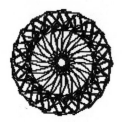

CLOSESPI 20 1 20

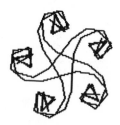

CLOSESPI 20 2 20

You may wish to experiment some more with this procedure. It can create many beautiful pictures.

In the next chapter, we will explore other methods for creating spirals, and these spirals will display dynamic symmetry.

X.

The Golden Mean

It may be argued that design may become an intellectual process, but it is just as important for the designer to understand the laws of harmoniously related forms and areas, as it is for the musical composer to be familiar with the laws of harmony and counterpoint.

(**from** Pattern and Design with Dynamic Symmetry, **Edward B. Edwards**)

With the single exception of squirals, the forms we have studied thus far have displayed static symmetry. In this chapter, we will explore one family of geometric forms that displays a dynamic symmetry based on the golden mean.

The origin of the golden mean is buried in antiquity. There is evidence that it was known to the Greek sculptor Phidias (c. 500 BC) and that it was used as a proportion in the construction of the Parthenon. By the 1500s, its appearance in mathematics became so commonplace that a book on the topic was published, with illustrations by Leonardo da Vinci. Since that time, numerous books and articles have been devoted to the appearance of the golden mean in nature and art. (The interested reader may wish to examine some of the books on this topic listed in the bibliography.)

The concept of the golden mean is quite simple: Divide a line into two segments so that the ratio of the longer to the shorter is the same as the ratio of the entire line to the longer segment. This ratio is the golden mean.

If we say that the shorter length is 1 unit long and that the longer segment is x units long, then the mathematical expression for the golden mean is

$$x = (x + 1)/x = \text{golden mean}$$

The value of x that satisfies this equation is $(\sqrt{5} + 1)/2$, which equals 1.61803. . . .

If we had chosen the shorter length to be x' and the longer portion to be 1, then we would find that

$$(1 + x') = 1/x'$$

The solution to this equation is $(\sqrt{5} - 1)/2$, which equals 0.61803. . . . Curiously, this value is exactly 1 less than the value of the golden mean. Furthermore (as you can easily verify), the golden mean has the property that, when diminished by 1, it becomes its own reciprocal. In other words,

$$1.61803 \ldots = 1/0.61803 \ldots$$

The golden mean is a number that appears to demonstrate an affinity for itself. It is as though, once you have it, nothing you do to it will make it go away.

The Magic Rectangle

Recall that we said that a figure displaying dynamic symmetry could be extended by applying the same rules that generated the figure in the first place. To see a graphic example of this phenomenon for the golden mean, we will start by constructing a golden rectangle—one whose length is 1.61803 . . . times longer than its height.

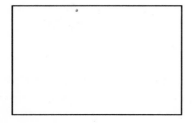

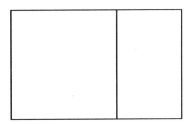

Rectangles with this aspect ratio often are spontaneously selected as being the most pleasing to the eye. Why our aesthetic sense should lead to this conclusion is a mystery. (You can test this result for yourself by constructing a series of rectangles ranging from a square to a rectangle with a ratio of 2:1 and asking people to select the most pleasing shape.)

Suppose that we say that the height of the rectangle is 1 unit. Its length is then 1.61803 . . . units. If we now draw a 1-unit square in this rectangle, we see that another rectangle is left over.

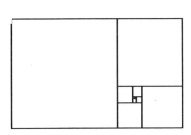

The short side of this rectangle is 0.61803 . . . units, and the long side is 1 unit. The ratio of the long to the short side is 1/0.61803 . . . , or the golden mean. In other words, if we subtract a square from a golden rectangle, we are left with another golden rectangle for a remainder. This process can be repeated indefinitely, with no change in the result.

The properties of this rectangle were studied by Jay Hambidge in the 1920s. He called it "the rectangle of the whirling squares." The following procedure will show why this name is so appropriate.

To create a procedure that generates a square we can write

```
TO SQUARE :SIZE
REPEAT 4 [FORWARD :SIZE RIGHT 90]
END
```

This generates a square that returns the turtle to its starting position.

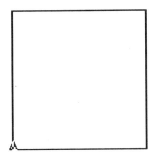

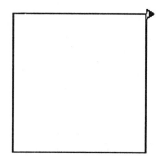

To add on to this figure, we need to move the turtle to an edge of the square. For the figure we desire, we need to move the turtle to the upper right corner and have it face to the right. This is most easily done by drawing the first two sides of the square over again.

Once we have moved the turtle to this new position, we want to draw another square that has sides 0.61803 . . . times smaller than the first square. As this procedure is repeated over and over again, we will generate the rectangle of the whirling squares.

```
TO WHIRL :SIZE
IF :SIZE < 1 [STOP]
REPEAT 4 [FORWARD :SIZE RIGHT 90]
FORWARD :SIZE RIGHT 90 FORWARD :SIZE
WHIRL :SIZE * 0.61803
END
```

As you can see, this procedure uses itself over and over again, with each new square being smaller than the previous one by a factor of 0.61803. . . .

To see the whirling squares, enter

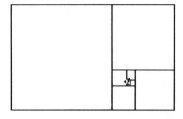

```
SHOWTURTLE
CLEARSCREEN
PENUP
SETPOS [ − 120 − 60]
PENDOWN
WHIRL 150
```

Next, imagine drawing a 90-degree arc connecting the two opposite corners of each square. As these arcs connect, they produce a spiral.

The proportional rule behind this spiral is that each segment is larger that its predecessor by the golden mean.

Spirals that grow by fixed ratios are common in

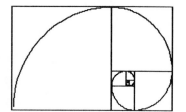

nature. They appear in snail shells, whirlpools, and numerous other natural objects and phenomena. Because of the various mathematical properties of such spirals, the same spiral can be called by different names. For example, because the angle at which the radius vector cuts the curve at any point is a constant, Descartes called it an equiangular spiral in 1638. Because of the proportional increase in its size, it has been called a proportional or geometric spiral. Bernoulli (who was so entranced by this figure that he had it engraved on his headstone in 1705) called it a logarithmic spiral. No matter what it is called, however, these names all refer to the same figure.

Spirals of this type can be approximated by a procedure that draws a series of 90-degree arcs for which each arc is larger than its predecessor by a fixed factor. There are two types of spirals—those that turn to the left and those that turn to the right. To generate a right-handed 90-degree arc, we can use the procedure

```
TO RARC :SIZE
REPEAT 30 [FORWARD :SIZE RIGHT 3]
END
```

And we can use this procedure for generating right-handed spirals by creating the procedure

```
TO RSPIRAL :STEPS :FACTOR
MAKE "SIZE 0.1
REPEAT :STEPS [RARC :SIZE MAKE "SIZE :SIZE *
    :FACTOR]
END
```

To generate left-handed spirals, we would use the procedures

```
TO LARC :SIZE
REPEAT 30 [FORWARD :SIZE LEFT 3]
END
```

```
TO LSPIRAL :STEPS :FACTOR
MAKE "SIZE 0.1
REPEAT :STEPS [LARC :SIZE MAKE "SIZE :SIZE *
   :FACTOR]
END
```

Next, we can experiment with spirals that use different expansion factors. If you enter

```
CLEARSCREEN
RSPIRAL 10 1
```

all you will see is a dot at the center of the screen. This is because you cannot increase the size of anything by multiplying it by 1. To see a spiral based on the golden mean, enter

```
WINDOW
CLEARSCREEN
PENUP SETPOS [−60 −   ] PENDOWN
RSPIRAL 10 1.61803
```

By increasing the size of the expansion factor, we can create spirals that are more open. For example, enter

```
CLEARSCREEN
RSPIRAL 10 2
```

To make a more tightly closed spiral, use numbers closer to 1, such as 1.2:

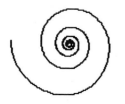

```
CLEARSCREEN
RSPIRAL 20 1.2
```

Interlaced spirals can be made by turning the turtle by different amounts before starting the spiral. For example, enter

```
CLEARSCREEN
LSPIRAL 15 1.5
```

This draws a left-handed spiral from the center of the screen. Next, we will change the pen color to blue and draw the same spiral from the center, but we will first turn the turtle by 180 degrees. Enter

```
PENUP HOME PENDOWN
SETPC 5
RIGHT 180
LSPIRAL 15 1.5
```

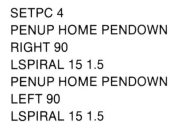

Notice that the blue spiral lies near the middle of the gap in the white spiral. To produce interwoven spirals with different locations, the same process can be repeated with other starting angles. The following example will add an orange line on either side of the blue one:

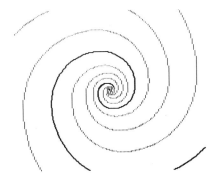

```
SETPC 4
PENUP HOME PENDOWN
RIGHT 90
LSPIRAL 15 1.5
PENUP HOME PENDOWN
LEFT 90
LSPIRAL 15 1.5
```

The Magic of Numbers and Fibonacci

Numerical series based on the golden mean were developed by the twelfth-century mathematician Leonardo Bigallo Fibonacci (also known as Leonardo da Pisa). In his travels to Algiers with his father, he learned about the golden mean and also learned the arabic number system, which he introduced to Europe.

The numerical series that bears his name is a simple additive series. Each number in the series is formed by adding the previous two numbers in the series. The Fibonacci series starts with the seed numbers 1 and 1. The first few numbers of this series are 1 1 2 3 5 8 13 21 34 55, and so on. One startling aspect of this series is its spontaneous appearance in nature. It is found, for example, in the interlocking spiral patterns of pinecones and sunflower seed clusters. In these structures, one can discern a set of right-handed and left-handed spiral arms. What is found is that the number of right- and left-handed arms are always two adjacent numbers in the Fibonacci series.

On a more aesthetic plane, one can *hear* the beauty of this series by assigning notes to each value. For example, if one assigned middle C to the number 1, D to the number 2, and so on, the first few notes of the Fibonacci series would look like the music shown here. By altering the syncopation and extending the melody, I have been able to create a Fibonacci Rag!

To see another amazing property of the Fibonacci series, we will first develop a Logo procedure that generates a list of Fibonacci numbers as long as we like. To do this, we must first understand some of the Logo primitives that work with words and lists. For example, suppose that we create a list:

MAKE ''ANIMALS [DOG CAT HORSE COW]

If we want to see the last item in the list, we could enter

PRINT LAST :ANIMALS

and see the word COW on the screen. To see the first item in the list, we enter

PRINT FIRST :ANIMALS

We can see all but the last item or all but the first item by entering

PRINT BUTLAST :ANIMALS

or

PRINT BUTFIRST :ANIMALS

The commands FIRST, LAST, BUTFIRST, and BUT-LAST can thus be used to take lists apart.

Lists can be put together in Logo by use of the SENTENCE command. For example, if we have a new animal, SHEEP, saved in the variable MORE:

MAKE "MORE "SHEEP

we can then add SHEEP to the list ANIMALS in this way:

MAKE "ANIMALS SENTENCE :ANIMALS :MORE

If you now enter

PRINT :ANIMALS

you will see the list

DOG CAT HORSE COW SHEEP

Using these commands, we can develop a strategy for building a series. We start with a seed series of at least two numbers and make a new number by adding the last number of the series to the next-to-last number. Finally, we extend the series by placing our new number at the very end of the seed. A two-member seed list will become a three-member list. Since we will want this new list to be the next seed, we need to be able to send its contents back out of the procedure. This is accomplished with the OUTPUT command. If a Logo procedure encounters a command such as

OUTPUT :SEED

then the current contents of the variable SEED is passed back out of the procedure, and the procedure stops execution.

If these concepts appear a bit vague, our example should help to clarify them. First, we will create a procedure that extends an additive series by one element each time it is used. Enter the following:

```
TO SERIES :SEED
MAKE "NEXT (LAST :SEED) + (LAST BUTLAST :SEED)
MAKE "SEED SENTENCE :SEED :NEXT
OUTPUT :SEED
END
```

To see what this procedure does, let's trace its execution line by line. First, the contents of NEXT is made to be the sum of the last element in SEED plus the next-to-last element (LAST BUTLAST :SEED). We used parentheses here to make sure that Logo would perform the operations properly and to make this line easier to read. Next, we place a new list in SEED, made from the old list with the new value (:NEXT) tagged on at the end. Finally, the modified list is passed back out of the procedure by the OUTPUT command.

To try this procedure, enter

SERIES [1 1]

The screen will show

I DON'T KNOW WHAT TO DO WITH [1 1 2]

This error message shows two things. First, we can see that the procedure works properly—[1 1 2] is the proper extension of [1 1], since the last element is the sum of the first two. Second, the error message shows that we need to do something with the list—we did not assign it to a word or do anything else with it. If we now enter

PRINT SERIES [1 1 2]

the display will show

1 1 2 3

We can use the **REPEAT** command to build a Fibonacci series of any length. For example, if you enter

MAKE "FSERIES [1 1]
REPEAT 20 [MAKE "FSERIES SERIES :FSERIES]

you will build 20 more terms into the series. To see the result, enter

PRINT :FSERIES

You should see the following list:

1 1 2 3 5 8 13 21 34 55 89 144 233 377 610 987 1597 2584
4181 6765 10946 17711

So far, we have found a way to build very long lists with numbers of the Fibonacci series. Next, we will do an experiment—dividing the last term in the series by the next-to-last term to see what we get. Here is a procedure that will do this for us:

```
TO RATIO :LIST
OUTPUT (LAST :LIST) / (LAST BUTLAST :LIST)
END
```

If we now enter

```
MAKE "FSERIES [1 1]
REPEAT 15 [MAKE "FSERIES SERIES :FSERIES]
PRINT RATIO :FSERIES
```

we will see the number **1.61803** typed on the screen! This number is the golden mean (to the accuracy of the computer's ability to perform calculations). Is this an accident? Let's expand the list some more—say, by ten more terms:

```
REPEAT 10 [MAKE "FSERIES SERIES :FSERIES]
PRINT RATIO :FSERIES
```

Once again we are presented, as if by magic, with the golden mean.

Of course, this doesn't hold for all terms in the series. For example, the ratio of the first two terms is 1:1, that of the third to the second is 2:1, and so on. This graph shows the ratios of successive elements for the first ten terms of the Fibonacci series.

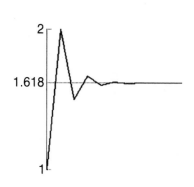

There are two interesting things to notice in this plot. First, the values of each ratio oscillate on either side of the golden mean. Second, the value of the ratio converges very quickly to a value very close to the golden mean.

Next, we can see a result that you might find quite surprising. Let's make an additive series using a seed of any two numbers. For example, enter

```
MAKE "SEED [ − 5 237]
```

Then create 20 more terms of the additive series by entering

REPEAT 20 [MAKE "SEED SERIES :SEED]

Can you guess what the ratio of the last two terms will be? If you enter

PRINT RATIO :SEED

you will see the number 1.61803.

No matter what two numbers are chosen as the seed value, the ratio of any two terms of an additive series will approach the golden mean. With such results, it is easy to see why the golden mean has captivated geometers and artists since antiquity.

XI.

How Long Is the Coast of California? Fractals and Recursion

As I was going to St. Ives,
I met a man with seven wives.
Each wife carried seven sacks;
And in each sack was seven cats;
And with each cat was seven kits.
Kits, cats, sacks, and wives,
How many were going to St. Ives?

Nursery Rhyme

How Long Is a Coastline?

This chapter deals with what appears to be a very simple question: How long is a coastline? One way to measure a coastline would be to use a map and a pair of dividers. Let's say that the map has a scale of one kilometer (km) of actual distance for each centimeter (cm) of distance on the map. If the dividers were set at a 10 cm spacing, a first approximation to the coast length could be obtained by counting the number of 10 cm steps along the coastline shown on the map and multiplying this number by 10 (since each 10 cm step corresponds to 10 km). In the process of measuring the coastline this way, however, we will have skipped over many details on the map—small bays, inlets, and the like.

To get a more accurate measure of coast length we might repeat the process with the dividers set at a 1 cm spacing. Because this finer setting would let us get into some (but not all) of the finer details along the coast, our calculated coast length (given by the number of 1 cm divider steps multiplied by 1) will be longer than our previous value. If we were now to use a more detailed map (one with a scale of 0.1 km per cm, for example), or if we were to use a smaller divider setting, we would pick up even more detail and thus obtain an even larger value for the coast length. In fact, the measured coastline increases as the measuring increment decreases. Imagine measuring around each rock outcropping and sand bank along the coast. This would produce an even longer coast length. And if we were to measure around each grain of sand at the water's edge, the number would be larger still.

And so the answer to the question "How long is the coast of California?" is "It depends."

It depends on what? It depends on the length of the measuring stick used in making the measurement. This is because the use of any measuring stick will result in a smoothing out of details that would have been measured if the stick were smaller.

Aside from being of obvious interest to mapmakers, problems of this sort have led to the creation of a new branch of mathematics called fractal geometry. Although the formal aspects of this geometry have their roots in work performed in the early 1900s, its detailed development resulted from the work of Benoit Mandelbrot in the 1950s. He coined the word *fractal* in 1975 to denote a mathematical set or concrete object whose form is extremely irregular and/or fragmented at all scales.

Our interest in fractals is twofold. First, many of the fractal curves are beautiful to look at. Second, simple Logo procedures can be written to describe these curves—curves that have defied traditional mathematical analysis and were considered monstrosities by early twentieth-century mathematicians.

Since many objects in the real world—from coastlines to blood vessels—are more accurately described by fractals than by smooth approximations, this field of mathematics will be receiving even more attention in the future.

Some Simple Fractal Curves

Let's start with a horizontal line one unit long. (The unit might be a kilometer, a centimeter, the length of your finger—it doesn't matter.)

This line represents our first approximation to a coastline we want to measure. Suppose that we now set the dividers to a spacing of ⅓ unit and measure the coast again. We might obtain this result.

This coastline has a triangular bump in it and is made from four lines, each of which is ⅓ unit in length. The total length of the coastline is now ⁴⁄₃ units.

Suppose that we now reduce the setting of the dividers to ⅓ of the previous setting and measure the coast again. What we discover (for this special coastline) is that each of the ⅓ unit straight lines is actually a replica of the coastline shown in the preceding figure. From this figure, we can see that each of the ⅓ unit lines is made of four lines, just as the preceding figure was. Since our new approximation has increased the length of each line by ⁴⁄₃ over its previous value, the new length of the coast is ⁴⁄₃ * ⁴⁄₃, or ¹⁶⁄₉ units long.

Suppose that we repeat this process again and discover that each of these straight line segments is in fact made from another four segments. This generates a coastline approximation that is ⁴⁄₃ * ⁴⁄₃ * ⁴⁄₃, or ⁶⁴⁄₂₇ units long—more than twice our original length.

What we have created is a very strange mathematical figure that has the property of increasing its length by $\frac{4}{3}$ each time we reduce the size of our measuring stick by $\frac{1}{3}$. If we continue this process indefinitely, we will end up with an infinitely long coastline that is pinned at both ends and around which we could draw a smooth boundary. Our strange figure is, in the limit, both infinitely long and infinitely bumpy.

This mathematical treat, called a triadic Koch curve, was discovered by H. von Koch in the early 1900s. Mathematicians of his day generally refused to study such "poorly behaved" functions. As we shall see, however, such functions are very easy to describe when using a computer language that supports recursive procedures.

Explicit Procedures for Drawing Fractals

Before developing a single recursive procedure for drawing approximations to the triadic Koch curve, we will explore some explicit methods that will help us understand the recursive form later.

The first procedures we will create are based on the second figure in this chapter. To draw this figure, we can use the following two procedures:

```
TO K0 :SIZE
FORWARD :SIZE
END

TO K1 :SIZE
K0 :SIZE / 3
LEFT 60
K0 :SIZE / 3
RIGHT 120
K0 :SIZE / 3
LEFT 60
K0 :SIZE / 3
END
```

(This may appear to be a hard way to draw the figure, but the power of this method will become obvious soon.)

To see the result of these procedures, we should start with the turtle near the left edge of the screen and facing to the right. The following setup procedure should do the job nicely:

```
TO SETUP
PENUP
SETPOS [ - 120  - 60]
PENDOWN
RIGHT 90
END
```

Now enter

```
CLEARSCREEN
SETUP
K1 243
```

(We chose 243 for the length of the curve because it fills the screen nicely and because it is a power of 3. The latter characteristic ensures that our more complex renditions of this figure will be drawn with integer line lengths.)

Suppose that we want to draw the next level of this curve. To do this, we need to replace each straight line segment with a replica of the figure generated by K1 with the value of **SIZE** reduced by a third. The following procedure does this for us:

```
TO K2 :SIZE
K1 :SIZE / 3
LEFT 60
K1 :SIZE / 3
RIGHT 120
K1 :SIZE / 3
LEFT 60
K1 :SIZE / 3
END
```

As you can see, K2 is identical to K1 except that K2 uses the procedure K1 and K1 uses the procedure K0. To see the result of this procedure, enter

```
CLEARSCREEN
SETUP
K2 243
```

By now, it should be pretty clear that we can generate the next level of the Koch curve by creating the procedure

```
TO K3 :SIZE
K2 :SIZE / 3
LEFT 60
K2 :SIZE / 3
RIGHT 120
K2 :SIZE / 3
LEFT 60
K2 :SIZE / 3
END
```

To see this level of the curve, enter

```
CLEARSCREEN
SETUP
K3 243
```

By making a simple modification to K3, we can create the procedure K4, which gives yet another level of detail to our figure. Once you have created K4, you should be able to generate this figure.

How far do we need to continue this process? We could easily create procedures up to K20 or so, but do we really need to? Since our original procedure, K1, drew lines that were 243/3, or 81 units long, the lines drawn by K2 were 27 units long. K3 used 9 unit lines, K4 used 3 units, and, if we were to define it, K5 would use lines 1 screen unit long. Since the Apple display screen can't handle lines less than 1 unit long, it hardly makes sense to try to create this curve with any more resolution than that.

This does not mean that the fractal curve can be accurately represented by only five levels of complexity. The true fractal triadic Koch curve uses infinitely many levels of procedures.

Because of Logo's ability to use recursion, we will be able to create a single compact procedure that represents the triadic Koch curve (or any other fractal) to any level of accuracy we wish.

Recursive Procedures for Drawing Fractals

If we look at procedures K0 through K4, we can see a clue that will show us how to create these fractal curves with only one procedure. The first thing to notice is that K0 is the only procedure that actually draws any lines. The other procedures only use lower-numbered procedures or turn the turtle. By writing the actual steps as they are executed, we can show how these procedures work. Let's examine K2, for example. If we expand the steps, we can see the sequence of commands as they are carried out. Each column in the following table shows a different procedure. Since K2 uses K1 and K1 uses K0, this table needs only three columns. The arrows show the direction in which control is passed from one procedure to the other.

TABLE OF COMMAND SEQUENCES FOR K2

K2	K1	K0

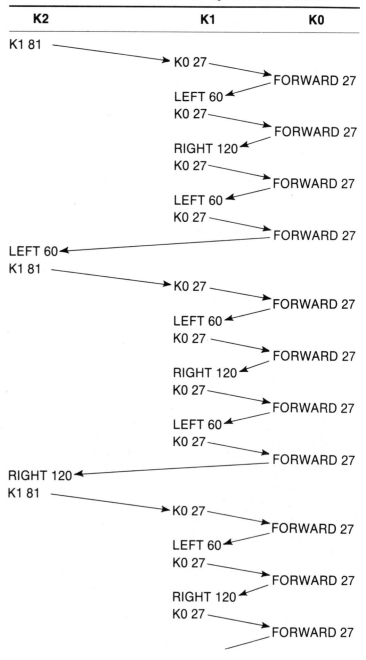

K1 81

        K0 27

                FORWARD 27

        LEFT 60

        K0 27

                FORWARD 27

        RIGHT 120

        K0 27

                FORWARD 27

        LEFT 60

        K0 27

                FORWARD 27

LEFT 60

K1 81

        K0 27

                FORWARD 27

        LEFT 60

        K0 27

                FORWARD 27

        RIGHT 120

        K0 27

                FORWARD 27

        LEFT 60

        K0 27

                FORWARD 27

RIGHT 120

K1 81

        K0 27

                FORWARD 27

        LEFT 60

        K0 27

                FORWARD 27

        RIGHT 120

        K0 27

                FORWARD 27

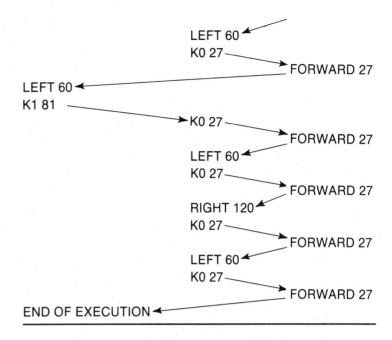

When we used **K2**, it used **K1** 4 times and **K1** used **K0** 16 times to actually draw the lines. A table for **K3** would be four times longer than this and would require four columns. If you decide to construct such a table yourself, you will see that, by the time **K3** has finished, it will have used **K2** 4 times, **K1** 16 times and **K0** 64 times.

Because of the similarities between **K1**, **K2**, **K3**, and so on, we should be able to use one procedure to create Koch curves with any level of complexity we want. We can do this because when Logo procedures use themselves recursively, Logo creates as many new copies of the procedure as are needed to keep the levels uniquely identified.

The only procedure we created that is markedly different from the rest is **K0**, because it only draws lines. The following procedure incorporates all the features of K0, K1, K2, and so on, into one compact form that lets us generate any level of triadic Koch curve we desire:

```
TO TRIAD :SIZE :LIMIT
IF :SIZE < :LIMIT [FORWARD :SIZE STOP]
TRIAD :SIZE / 3 :LIMIT
LEFT 60
TRIAD :SIZE / 3 :LIMIT
RIGHT 120
TRIAD :SIZE / 3 :LIMIT
LEFT 60
TRIAD :SIZE / 3 :LIMIT
END
```

To see how this procedure operates, let's examine it line by line. Suppose that you gave the command **TRIAD 243 100**, for example. First, the size (**243**) would be tested to see if it is less than the limit (**100**). Because it is not, **TRIAD** would be used again with a size of 243/3, or 81. Since, in this new use of **TRIAD**, the size (**81**) is less than 100, a line will be drawn (just as with the K0 procedure). As soon as this happens, the **STOP** command forces Logo back to the earlier version of **TRIAD** to carry out its next command (**LEFT 60**). This process is continued in just the same way that K1 used K0. The only difference is that we are taking advantage of Logo's ability to keep track of multiple uses of a procedure that we have defined only once. It is as though Logo makes as many copies of **TRIAD** as it needs and gives them special names so that they are used in the right order.

The concept of recursive programming is probably the trickiest and most powerful concept you will encounter as you use computers. If you are confused by recursion, you may want to reexamine the previous section before exploring the next examples.

As a measure of recursion's power, notice that TRIAD can be used to describe any level of approximation to the triadic Koch curve. The ten-line procedure is all that is needed to describe a mathematical curve that was avoided by many mathematicians for years!

Experiment with TRIAD (leaving the turtle visible). By watching the figure being drawn, you might gain more insight into the way that recursion is being used to create the figure. To generate the figures we have already drawn, you might use

```
TRIAD 243 243
TRIAD 243 81
TRIAD 243 27
TRIAD 243 9
```

Remember to clear the screen and use SETUP before drawing each curve. To see the most detailed level of this curve that can be shown on the screen, enter

```
CLEARSCREEN
SETUP
TRIAD 243 3
```

Fractals can be generated from any pattern that can be used in a self-replicating manner. For example, suppose that we use a square-cornered figure instead of the triangular one we used previously.

Since each of the five lines used in this figure is one-third the span of the pattern from left to right, we can generate the next-level curve by repeating this pattern in place of each straight line segment. The following procedure lets us generate this curve to any level of complexity we desire:

```
TO QUADRIC :SIZE :LIMIT
IF :SIZE < :LIMIT [FORWARD :SIZE STOP]
QUADRIC :SIZE / 3 :LIMIT
```

```
LEFT 90
QUADRIC :SIZE / 3 :LIMIT
RIGHT 90
QUADRIC :SIZE / 3 :LIMIT
RIGHT 90
QUADRIC :SIZE / 3 :LIMIT
LEFT 90
QUADRIC :SIZE / 3 :LIMIT
END
```

To see the patterns that result from this fractal procedure, try these values (remembering to clear the screen and use **SETUP** before each figure is drawn):

QUADRIC 243 243

QUADRIC 243 81

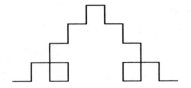

QUADRIC 243 27

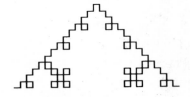

QUADRIC 243 9

QUADRIC 243 3

It is interesting that an exploration of the length of a coastline could lead us to a pattern that would look more at home on a lace napkin.

To see a completely closed pattern based on this figure (a quadric Koch island), enter the following procedure:

```
TO ISLAND :SIZE :LIMIT
REPEAT 4 [QUADRIC :SIZE :LIMIT RIGHT 90]
END
```

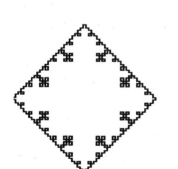

Now you can create a complete closed figure by entering

```
CLEARSCREEN
PENUP SETPOS [−20 −30] PENDOWN
ISLAND 81 9
```

Does it surprise you to know that the turtle's net turning for this figure is 360 degrees?

In the next chapter, we will explore a few more examples of recursive procedures.

XII.

Trees and Other Subjects

I think that I shall never see
A procedure lovely as a tree.
But unless I master the recursive call,
I'll never see a tree at all.

Trees and Branching

The types of fractal curves we examined in the last chapter represent only a small sampling of the myriad geometric forms that are built from copies of a master unit. If you examine a tree, for example, you can see a single large trunk that carries several large branches, each of which carries smaller branches, and so on. Finally, from small twigs, we see clusters of leaves. In many ways, this description of a tree suggests that we can use a recursive Logo procedure to draw them.

Let's start, for example, with a simple forked pattern of new branches that would appear at the end of each older branch.

Our challenge is to define a procedure that will create a pattern of branches whose ends each contain the same branching pattern, reduced in size by some factor.

A simple branch pair can be constructed by a simple procedure that leaves the turtle in the same position in which it started:

```
TO BRANCH :SIZE
LEFT 45
FORWARD :SIZE
BACK :SIZE
```

```
RIGHT 90
FORWARD :SIZE
BACK :SIZE
LEFT 45
END
```

This procedure draws the first branch and then comes back to the origin before drawing the second branch. After the second branch is drawn, the turtle returns to the origin and orients itself to its original position. To replicate this pattern at the end of each branch tip, we need to repeat the branching process when the turtle has reached the end of each previous branch. The following procedure is very similar to **BRANCH** but contains some important differences:

```
TO TREE :SIZE :LIMIT
IF :SIZE < :LIMIT [STOP]
LEFT 45
FORWARD :SIZE
TREE :SIZE * 0.61803 :LIMIT
BACK :SIZE
RIGHT 90
FORWARD :SIZE
TREE :SIZE * 0.61803 :LIMIT
BACK :SIZE
LEFT 45
END
```

The differences between **TREE** and **BRANCH** are, first, that **TREE** is used recursively at the end of each branch. The sizes of the recursive branches are each reduced by a factor of 0.61803 from the length of the previous branch. You can use any factor you wish in place of this value. For example, a value of 0.5 will make the new branches half as long as the previous ones. The factor we have chosen (based on the golden mean) makes a very pretty tree (as we shall soon see). The other major difference between **TREE** and **BRANCH** is the test to check if :SIZE is less than :LIMIT. This test serves the same purpose it did for our fractal procedures in the last chapter. This type of conditional expression is needed in all recursive procedures of this type.

　　To generate a display of our simple tree, enter

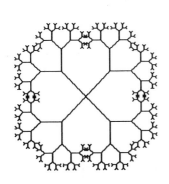

```
WINDOW
CLEARSCREEN
PENUP SETY −40 PENDOWN
TREE 64 2
BACK 64
```

As this figure is being drawn, you can see clearly the various levels of recursion being used to generate the tree. The last command (**BACK 64**) provides our tree with a trunk.

　　If you study the picture generated by **TREE 64 2** closely, you may see a recursive family of hearts formed by the intertwining branches. As pretty as this picture is, it is far too symmetrical to look very realistic. However, one could use this pattern to generate an interesting Valentine picture by entering

```
CLEARSCREEN
REPEAT 2 [TREE 50 2 RIGHT 180]
```

　　How do we generate a more realistic looking tree? Our first example underwent branching at exactly the same point on both branches. In real trees, this is highly unlikely.

　　Suppose that we designed a procedure that used a simple two-element branch for which the left arm was twice as long as the right arm. This is still far from realistic, but it gives us an interesting pattern.

Instead of reducing the size of the branches as the tree grows, we can leave them the same size to see what effect this has on the final pattern. An unfortunate consequence of this approach is that we can no longer examine the branch size to determine which level of recursion we are using, so we will use a simple counter for this purpose. Enter the following procedure:

```
TO FTREE :SIZE :COUNTER
IF :COUNTER = 0 [STOP]
LEFT 30
FORWARD :SIZE * 2
FTREE :SIZE :COUNTER − 1
BACK :SIZE * 2
RIGHT 60
FORWARD :SIZE
FTREE :SIZE :COUNTER − 1
BACK :SIZE
LEFT 30
END
```

If you trace the operation of this procedure, you can see its similarities to the previous **TREE** procedure.

To see the pattern generated by this procedure, enter

```
CLEARSCREEN
WINDOW
PENUP SETY − 40 PENDOWN
FTREE 20 5
BACK 40
```

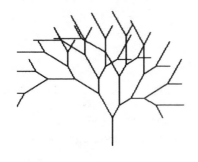

This is a far more realistic looking tree because of its apparent asymmetry. Some branches cross over others, and the tree leans a bit off center—much as a real tree might.

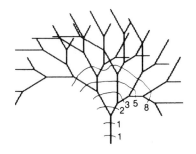

It so happens that this tree has another interesting property. Let us suppose that the growth rate for both branches is the same, so that the longer branch takes twice as long to grow as the shorter one. We can then draw contour lines of equal growth for this tree and count the number of branches crossed by each contour line.

When we do this, we are presented with the series 1 1 2 3 5 8 . . . —the Fibonacci series! The procedure **FTREE** creates a Fibonacci tree. Thus we see yet another example of this series' spontaneous appearance in nature and mathematics.

Random Motions

Thus far, we have presented illustrations that suggest the presence of a tremendous amount of order in the universe. It is only fair that we devote at least some time to chaos, since chaos is the wellspring from which all order arises. Just as Logo is an appropriate language for the exploration of symmetry, it can let us study randomness as well. The principal tool for this is the operation RANDOM. If you enter the command

PRINT RANDOM 100

a number between 0 and 99 will be typed on the screen. Each time RANDOM is used, it randomly picks an integer from 0 to one less than the limit specified.

The easiest way to explore random motions is to have the turtle "walk" around the screen in fixed-length steps. After each step, the turtle is randomly pointed in another direction. For example, enter

WINDOW
CLEARSCREEN
SHOWTURTLE
REPEAT 50 [FORWARD 10 RIGHT RANDOM 360]

As you can see, the turtle is buffeted about as it moves. The path it creates is quite confused. This type of motion is characteristic of small dust particles buffeted by the random motions of air molecules. It is called Brownian motion, after its discoverer.

It is this random motion of molecules that results in the ultimately uniform dispersal of a drop of ink in a glass of water. To see the result of random motion for a particle constrained to be on the display screen, enter

WRAP
CLEARSCREEN
REPEAT 1000 [FORWARD 10 RIGHT RANDOM 360]

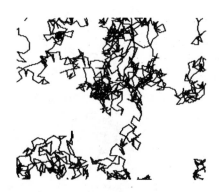

As you can see, some areas of the screen are covered quite thoroughly, while others are left open. Yet, if we allowed the process to continue indefinitely, we would find that the turtle was equally likely to have covered any screen location.

One limitation of the fractal coastlines we explored in the preceding chapter is that, like our first tree, they are too symmetrical. Real coastlines (or mountain ranges) appear to be far more random in their appearance.

Whether or not mountain ranges *are* random is beside the point, however. Their appearance of randomness allows us to create a procedure for drawing mountain ranges.

The randomness of mountain tops is of a special sort. Clearly, the angles of the bumps are not so unconstrained as to make them look like the path of a particle undergoing Brownian motion. Also, the jagged outline of the mountains appears to use sides of varying lengths. This suggests that a procedure for drawing mountain ranges should use two sorts of randomness—a limited randomness in the direction of the drawn line and a limited randomness in the length of the drawn line.

If our mountains were perfectly flat, the turtle's heading would always be 90 degrees. The bumpiness of the mountain range is determined by the extent to which the angles are allowed to vary around this value. The following procedure lets us create mountain ranges with different amounts of bumpiness:

```
TO MOUNTAINS :BUMP
PENUP SETHEADING 90 BACK 120 PENDOWN
REPEAT 60 [SETHEADING ( (90 − :BUMP) + RANDOM
  (2 * :BUMP) ) FORWARD RANDOM 15]
END
```

These figures were generated with different amounts of bumpiness. (Remember to clear the screen before drawing each mountain range.)

```
WINDOW
CLEARSCREEN
MOUNTAINS 0


MOUNTAINS 15


MOUNTAINS 30


MOUNTAINS 60


MOUNTAINS 90
```

Depending on where you live, you might be able to see a silhouette of mountains on the horizon that appears similar to one of these figures.

The use of random numbers in geometry allows us to create many patterns that closely represent some aspects of the world around us. Harmony coexists with chaos, and mastery of both is essential for even a partial understanding of the universe.

XIII.

Conclusion: The Tyranny of Space

All patterns, whether drawn by artists, calculated by mathematicians, or produced by natural forces are shaped by the same spatial environment. All are subject to the tyranny of space. Synthetic patterns of lines and dots are engaging in their own right but, more importantly, they speak eloquently of the order that all things inevitably share.

(from Patterns in Nature, **Peter Stevens)**

There have been several observations made in this book that appear to be universally true. We have seen, for example, that any simple planar closed path results in a total turning angle of 360 degrees. We have seen that the sum of the interior angles around any node of a tesselation must equal 360 degrees. We have seen several examples of the spontaneous appearance of the golden mean.

Yet these observations are only true for the dimensionalities of space in which we exist. But just what is the dimensionality of our space?

We think of ourselves as living in a three-dimensional world—a world in which physical objects have height, breadth, and depth. Because of our comprehension of three-dimensional space, it is easy for us to understand spaces with fewer dimensions (for example, two), but it is harder for us to develop intuitions regarding spaces with more dimensions (for example, four).

Because we think of the three dimensions of our experience as lines, areas, and volumes, one might assume that the only dimensions we have are given by the integers 1, 2, and 3. For example, we can say that a three-dimensional volume is characterized by the fact that if two parallel surfaces are brought arbitrarily close together within this volume, there would be "volume" between the surfaces for any arbitrary separation. Similarly, two parallel one-dimensional lines can be brought arbitrarily close to each other on a two-dimensional surface and there will still be "surface" between them. Finally, two zero-dimensional points can be brought arbitrarily close to each other on a one-dimensional line and there would still be "line" between them. This model of dimensionality was well known to philosophers such as Aristotle and has profoundly influenced the way we think about our universe. We often think of objects as having surfaces and volumes, and we often talk about connecting points with lines. We must ask, however, if this restriction to integer dimensions (and the corresponding labels of line, surface, and volume) is relevant to the real world. What, for example, is the surface of a sponge? What is its volume? Do we define a sponge's surface as the area of a sheet of smooth material that just covers it? Alternatively, we must examine the surface area of the pores that characterize the sponge's squishiness. If we go too far in that direction, however, we might decide that a sponge is mostly surface, with almost no volume. The trade-off between apparent surface and apparent volume for physical objects like sponges suggests that a mathematical model of a sponge might benefit from the use of other dimensions. As pleasing as the concept of integer dimensions might be (along with the corresponding concepts of line, surface, and volume), we should feel free to broaden our concept of dimension to include dimensions that are nonintegers and that are not pure lines, surfaces, or volumes. Without knowing it, we have already encountered figures with noninteger dimensions—the fractals.

To understand this concept, we must first develop a general expression for dimensionality. This general expression will have the property of being consistent with our intuitions regarding lines, surfaces, and volumes, but will also free us to examine other dimensions.

Consider, first, a one-dimensional straight line of 1 unit length that has been divided into N equal pieces of length r.

We can see that

$$N = (1/r)$$

As r is decreased, N increases linearly—the expected result for a one-dimensional line.

Next, let us examine a two-dimensional square of 1 unit length that has been divided into N equal subsquares of length r.

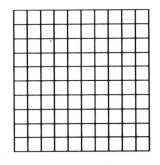

From this figure we can see that

$$N = (1/r)^2$$

As r is decreased, N increases by the second power of $1/r$—the expected result for a two-dimensional figure. You can easily see that a similar result holds true for the cube (using the third power). What we have found is that the exponent of this equation corresponds to the dimension of the object we are dividing into N pieces.

In general, we can state that

$$N = (1/r)^D$$

in which D is the dimensionality of the object under study. By taking the logarithm of both sides of the equation, we find that

$$\log N = D \log (1/r)$$

and, by rearranging the terms, that the dimensionality is given by

$$D = \log N / \log (1/r)$$

Now let's apply this result to the two fractal curves we examined in Chapter XI.

The triadic Koch curve is based on this figure.

Each time the length of our measuring unit (r) is reduced by a factor of 3, the number of separate segments increases by 4. We can see this by counting the segments for the first few levels of division. We start with 4 segments. When we divide the length by 3, the number of segments increases to 16. When we divide by 3 again, the number increases to 64. If this curve were one-dimensional, then each time we divided it by 3, the number of segments would increase by 3. If it were two-dimensional, then the number of segments would increase by 3 to the second power, or 9. Since the number of segments actually increases by 4, we can begin to develop an intuitive feeling for the idea that this curve has a dimension intermediate between 1 and 2. In fact, for this figure, $N = 4$ and $r = \frac{1}{3}$. Thus,

$$D = \log 4 / \log 3 = 1.2619. \ldots$$

This curve has a dimensionality somewhere between that of a line and an area. As a result, it is neither a line nor an area, but something else altogether. Because the dimension is fairly close to 1, we might say that this curve is more like a line than it is like an area, but what does that really mean?

The second curve we explored was the quadric fractal based on this figure.

For this figure, a reduction of r by ⅓ results in the number of segments increasing by a factor of 5. This curve has a dimension given by

$$D = \log 5 \,/\, \log 3 = 1.4650. \ldots$$

We can say that this second curve is closer to a two-dimensional figure than is the first. This is confirmed by our own observation when the two fractals are compared. The second figure appears to fill more area than the first.

Perhaps one way to further understand the nature of fractional dimensions is to explore a fractal with a dimension of 2. The following procedure generates one example of a two-dimensional fractal:

```
TO TWODIM :SIZE :LIMIT
IF :SIZE < :LIMIT [FORWARD :SIZE STOP]
TWODIM :SIZE / 2 :LIMIT
LEFT 90
TWODIM :SIZE / 2 :LIMIT
RIGHT 180
TWODIM :SIZE / 2 :LIMIT
LEFT 90
TWODIM :SIZE / 2 :LIMIT
END
```

To see the patterns that result from this fractal procedure, try these values (remembering to clear the screen and use the **SETUP** procedure we defined in Chapter XI before each figure is drawn):

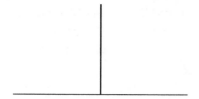

TWODIM 256 256

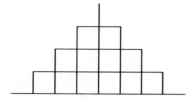

TWODIM 256 64

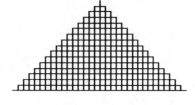

TWODIM 256 16

TWODIM 256 4

These figures clearly illustrate the emerging transition from a simple set of lines to a completely covered area as the number of segments is allowed to increase. As each level of the curve is generated, it adds lines between those also generated at earlier levels. Ultimately, as the number of segments increases without bound, we achieve complete surface coverage with this fractal.

Perhaps you are beginning to feel more comfortable with the concept of noninteger dimensions. It is a concept that is so new and strange that it might take a few weeks for it to make sense to you. As you can see, however, our arbitrary restriction of dimensions to the integers is inadequate to describe either nature or certain objects in mathematics.

If space can accommodate fractals, then what about time? Does time have fractal characteristics? Remember that one aspect of fractal figures is that they get longer as our measuring stick gets shorter. Our subjective experience with time is very reminiscent of this. An hour spent at a concert or ball game can seem like a few minutes, but the four minutes spent watching a clock while taking a child's temperature can seem like an hour. Our subjective exposure to the fractal aspects of time is well expressed by the saying "A watched pot never boils."

Each of us has a lifetime of experience with subjective time intervals. Some short events take forever (it seems), and some long events are over too soon. Our use of mechanical time-measuring devices gives an order to our existence that would be missing if we each operated on our own time scheme. Even before the invention of the clock, we used the sun, moon, seasons, and stars to provide us with measures of days, months, quarters, and years. But suppose that we had no clocks, and suppose that we were fixed in space along with the sun, moon, and stars. What would time be for us then? Perhaps the rhythm of our heartbeats and breathing would provide us with another system for measuring time. Would the short intervals of these events cause us to think of time as "taking longer"?

As with so many aspects of the universe in which we live, there are no easy answers to these questions. Perhaps it is enough to be able to ask the questions and to speculate on their answers. That has been one of the goals of this book—and it is one of the appropriate uses of Logo.

I have chosen to call this chapter a conclusion, but it is far from that. Some of the subjects we have introduced have enchanted people for millenia, and they promise to do so for thousands of years to come.

If some of these topics have stimulated your interest in pattern and mathematics, then you are on the path to making your own discoveries of beauty.

Bibliography

The following list should serve as a brief introduction to the books on the listed topics. Although it is far from complete, this list should provide a useful starting point for further exploration.

Turtle Geometry and User-Friendly Computer Languages

H. Abelson, *Logo for the Apple II*, Byte Books/McGraw-Hill, 1982.

H. Abelson and A. diSessa, *Turtle Geometry: The Computer as a Medium for Exploring Mathematics*, MIT Press, 1981.

S. Papert, *Mindstorms: Children, Computers, and Powerful Ideas*, Basic Books, 1980.

D. D. Thornburg, *Every Kid's First Book of Robots and Computers*, Compute Books, 1982.

D. D. Thornburg, *Picture This! An Introduction to Computer Graphics for Kids of All Ages*, Addison-Wesley, 1982.

D. D. Thornburg, *Picture This Too! An Introduction to Computer Graphics for Kids of All Ages*, Addison-Wesley, 1982.

Polygons and Polyhedra

H. S. M. Coxeter, *Regular Polytopes*, Dover Publications, 1973.

R. B. Fuller, *Synergetics*, Macmillan, 1975.

R. B. Fuller, *Synergetics 2*, Macmillan, 1979.

H. Kenner, *Geodesic Math and How to Use It*, University of California Press, 1976.

P. Pearce and S. Pearce, *Polyhedra Primer*, Van Nostrand Reinhold, 1978.

A. Pugh, *An Introduction to Tensegrity*, University of California Press, 1976.

A. Pugh, *Polyhedra: A Visual Approach*, University of California Press, 1976.

Static Symmetry

S. Kim, *Inversions*, Byte Books/McGraw-Hill, 1981.

J. F. Nye, *Physical Properties of Crystals*, Oxford University Press, 1967.

F. Phillips, *An Introduction to Crystallography*, Wiley, 1963.

P. Stevens, *Handbook of Regular Patterns: An Introduction to Symmetry in Two Dimensions*, MIT Press, 1981.

Dynamic Symmetry

G. Doczi, *The Power of Limits: Proportional Harmonies in Nature, Art and Architecture*, Shambala Press, 1981.

E. B. Edwards, *Pattern and Design with Dynamic Symmetry*, Dover Publications, 1967.

M. Ghyka, *The Geometry of Art and Life*, Dover Publications, 1977.

J. Hambidge, *The Elements of Dynamic Symmetry*, Dover Publications, 1967.

H. E. Huntley, *The Divine Proportion: A Study in Mathematical Beauty*, Dover Publications, 1970.

Tessellations

S. Bezuszka, M. Kenney, and L. Silvey, *Tessellations: The Geometry of Patterns*, Creative Publications, 1977.

C. Macgillavry, *Fantasy and Symmetry: The Periodic Drawings of M. C. Escher*, Abrams, 1976.

E. R. Ranucci and J. L. Teeters, *Creating Escher-Type Drawings*, Creative Publications, 1977.

Fractals

R. L. Knowles, *Energy and Form*, MIT Press, 1974. (of related interest)

B. B. Mandelbrot, *Fractals: Form, Chance, and Dimension*, W. H. Freeman, 1977.

B. B. Mandelbrot, *The Fractal Geometry of Nature*, W. H. Freeman, 1982.

Patterns in Nature, Artifacts, Myth, and Religion

G. Bateson, *Mind and Nature—A Necessary Unity*, Dutton, 1979.

C. Jung, *Man and His Symbols*, Aldus Books, 1964.

P. Pearce, *Structure in Nature Is a Strategy for Design*, MIT Press, 1978.

P. Pearce and S. Pearce, *Experiments in Form—A Foundation Course in Three-Dimensional Design*, Van Nostrand Reinhold, 1980.

N. Rennick, *Sacred Geometry*, Harper & Row, 1982.

P. S. Stevens, *Patterns in Nature*, Atlantic–Little, Brown, 1974.

Recursion

D. R. Hofstadter, *Gödel, Escher, Bach: An Eternal Golden Braid*, Basic Books, 1979.

D. D. Thornburg, *Discovering Apple Logo: An Invitation to the Art and Pattern of Nature*, Addison-Wesley, 1983.

Index

Other books in the Microcomputer Books Series, available from your local computer store or bookstore. For more information write:

General Books Division
Addison-Wesley Publishing Company, Inc.
Reading, Massachusetts 01867
(617) 944-3700

(07768)   **Picture This! An Introduction to Computer Graphics for Kids of All Ages**
David D. Thornburg

(10113)   **Computer Choices**
H. Dominic Covvey and Neil Harding McAlister

(10341)   **Pascal: A Problem Solving Approach**
Elliot B. Koffman

(10939)   **Computer Consciousness**
H. Dominic Covvey and Neil Harding McAlister

(03115)   **A Bit of BASIC**
Thomas A. Dwyer and Margot Critchfield

(01589)   **BASIC and the Personal Computer**
Thomas A. Dwyer and Margot Critchfield

(05247)   **The Little Book of BASIC Style**
John M. Nevison

(05248)   **Executive Computing**
John M. Nevison

(03399)   **The S6800 Family: Hardware Fundamentals**
Mitchell Goozé

(01937)   **Real Time Programming: Neglected Topics**
Caxton C. Foster

(01995)   **Programming A Microcomputer: 6502**
Caxton C. Foster

(07773)   **Interfacing Microcomputers to the Real World**
Murray Sargent III and Richard L. Shoemaker

(10187)   **How to Choose Your Small Business Computer**
Mark Birnbaum and John Sickman

(05735)   **Low-Cost Word Processing**
Laurence Press

(10242)   **Executive VisiCalc for the Apple Computer**
Roger E. Clark

(07767)   **Picture This Too!**
David D. Thornburg

(06192)   **The Computer Image**
Donald Greenberg, Aaron Marcus, Allan Schmidt, and Vernon Gorter

(10158)   **Pascal From BASIC**
Peter Brown

(10355)   **CP/M and the Personal Computer**
Thomas A. Dwyer and Margot Critchfield

(10243)   **Executive VisiCalc for the IBM Personal Computer**
Roger E. Clark

(05092)   **Microcomputer Graphics**
Roy E. Myers

(06577)   **Pascal for BASIC Programmers**
Charles Seiter and Robert Weiss